HEROES OF HISTORY

HEROES OF HISTORY_{BY}
WINSTON CHURCHILL

PICTURES BY ROBERT MAC LEAN

*A Selection
of Churchill's
Favourite Historical Characters
All Told in His Own Words
from his four-volume* A HISTORY
OF THE ENGLISH-SPEAKING
PEOPLES *Followed by a profile
of Sir Winston himself
Drawn from
autobiographical
writings and
speeches*

CASSELL AND COMPANY LTD

London

EDITOR'S NOTE

What manner of man was Winston Churchill! Orator, statesman, warrior, painter—and, not least, writer. He has said in telling of his early years, "I got into my bones the essential structure of the ordinary English sentence—which is a noble thing." How noble, the readers of this book will find, to their pleasure and inspiration, on every page.

For Winston Churchill, history was no dead recital of things past. It was real and living—and above all, it was about people. *And for him, cast in the heroic mould, it was the heroes of history who gave life and reality to the fabric of events.*

Here, then, are thirteen of Sir Winston's favourite characters in history— kings and queens, soldiers and sailors, saints and statesmen. Their stories are told in his own incomparable words from the pages of his four-volume HISTORY. This means inevitably in so long a work that much of his explanatory material has been left out. This background is presented, where it has seemed necessary, in marginal notes. And to complete the picture, there is a profile of Sir Winston, himself perhaps the greatest hero of them all, drawn from his own autobiographical writings and from his speeches.

CASSELL & COMPANY LTD
35 Red Lion Square, London WC1
Melbourne, Sydney, Toronto
Johannesburg, Auckland

Quotations from Winston Churchill's MY EARLY LIFE: A Roving Commission and THOUGHTS AND ADVENTURES are reprinted by permission of the Hamlyn Publishing Group.

CONTENTS

ALFRED THE GREAT

849-901

THE BATTLE OF ASHDOWN

THE "GREAT HEATHEN ARMY"

HALFDENE

GUTHRUM

THE BATTLE OF ETHANDUN

THE *SAXON CHRONICLE*

EDWARD

HAESTEN

ALFRED is known to us in some detail for his religious and moral qualities, but we must also remember that, in spite of ill-health, he was renowned as a hunter, and that his father had taken him to Rome as a boy, so that he had a lively comprehension of the great world. Alfred began as second-in-command to his elder brother, King Ethelred. There were no jealousies between them, but a marked difference of temperament. Ethelred inclined to the religious view that faith and prayer were the prime agencies by which the heathen would be overcome. Alfred, though also devout, laid the emphasis upon policy and arms.

The Danes had occupied London, not then the English capital, but a town in the kingdom of Mercia, and their army had fortified itself at Reading. Moving forward, they met the forces of the Saxons on the Berkshire downs, and here, in January 871, was fought the Battle of Ashdown. Both sides divided their forces into two commands. Ethelred tarried long at his devotions. The Vikings, with their brightly painted shields and banners, their finery and golden bracelets, made the Saxons seem modest by contrast. As they slowly approached they clashed their shields and weapons and raised long, repeated, and defiant war-cries. Although archery was not much in use, missiles began to fly. The King was still at his prayers. God came first, he declared to those who warned him that the battle must soon be joined. But Alfred seeing the heathen had come quickly on to the field and were ready for battle could bear the attacks of the enemy no longer. At last, like a wild boar, he led the Christian forces boldly against the army of the enemy in spite of the fact that the King had not yet arrived.

The fight was long and hard. King Ethelred, his spiritual duty done, soon joined his brother. There was in that place a single stunted thorn-tree which we have seen with our own eyes. Round about this tree, then, the opposing ranks met in conflict, with a great shouting from all men —one side bent on evil, the other side fighting for life and their loved ones and their native land. At last the Danes gave way, and, hotly pursued, fled back to Reading. They

After the Romans withdrew from Britain around A.D. 425, the island was invaded periodically by Nordic tribes who mixed with the native Celts and Gaels. Later on, these combined peoples were called Angles and Saxons. In 787 the Danes started a series of raids lasting a hundred years until the time of Alfred.

Churchill uses the names Danes and Vikings interchangeably.

ENGLAND
871
Strathclyde
Northumbria
Wales
Mercia
East Anglia
Wessex
London
Reading
Ashdown

7

fled till nightfall; they fled through the night and the next day, and the whole breadth of the Berkshire hills was strewn with their corpses.

The results of this victory did not break the power of the Danish army; in a fortnight they were again in the field. But the Battle of Ashdown justly takes its place among historic encounters because of the greatness of the issue. If the West Saxons had been beaten all England would have sunk into heathen anarchy. Since they were victorious the hope still burned for a civilised Christian existence in this Island. This was the first time the invaders had been beaten in the field. Alfred had made the Saxons feel confidence in themselves again. They could hold their own in open fight. The story of this conflict at Ashdown was for generations a treasured memory. It was Alfred's first battle.

King Ethelred soon fell sick and died. Although he had young children there was no doubt who his successor must be. At twenty-four Alfred became King, and entered upon a desperate inheritance. To and fro the fighting swayed, with varying fortunes. Seven or eight battles were fought, and we are told the Danes usually held the field. In the summer, about a month after Alfred assumed the crown, he sustained a definite defeat in the heart of his own country. His numbers had been worn down by death and desertion, and once again in the field the Vikings' ruse of a feigned retreat was successful.

The tribute money, usually gold, paid to the Danes for a period of peace was called "Danegeld."

On the morrow of this misfortune Alfred thought it best to come to terms while he still had an army. We do not know the conditions, but there is no doubt that a heavy payment of "Danegeld" was among them. By this inglorious treaty and stubborn campaign Alfred secured five years in which to consolidate his power.

The reasons which led the Danes to make a truce with Alfred are hard to analyse at this date. They were certainly convinced that only by prolonged and bloody fighting could they master the Saxons. Both sides liked war, and this had been ding-dong; there was little to show but scars and corpses on either side. But Alfred had al-

ways counted upon the invaders dividing, and the stresses
at work within the heathen army justified his policy.

But now in the last quarter of the century a subtle,
profound change came over the "Great Heathen Army."
Alfred and the men of Wessex had proved too stubborn a
foe for easy subjugation. Some of the Danes wished to settle on the lands they already held; the rest were for contin-
uing the war at a suitable moment till the whole country
was conquered. Thus nearly half of the sea-pirates settled
themselves in Northumbria and East Anglia. Henceforward
they began "to till the ground for a livelihood." Here was
a great change. We must remember their discipline and
organisation. The ships' companies, acting together, had
hitherto fought ashore as soldiers. All their organisation
of settlements was military. The sailors had turned soldiers,
and the soldiers had turned yeomen. They preserved that
spirit of independence, regulated only by comradeship and
discipline for vital purposes, which was the life of the
long-ship.

The district of Wessex was the seat of Alfred's power.

The whole of the East of England thus received a class
of cultivator who, except for purposes of common defence,
owed allegiance to none; who had won his land with the
sword, and was loyal only to the army organisation which
enabled him to keep it. This sturdy, upstanding stock took
root. As time passed they forgot the sea; they forgot the
army; they thought only of the land—their own land.
They liked the life. Although they were sufficiently skillful
agriculturists there was nothing they could teach the older
inhabitants; they brought no new implements or methods,
but they were resolved to learn.

The distribution of the land was made around a unit
which could support a family. What eight oxen could
plough in a certain time under prescribed conditions became the measure of the holding. They worked hard themselves, but obviously they used the local people too.

Thus the Danish differs in many ways from the Saxon
settlements four hundred years earlier. There was no idea
of exterminating the older population. The two languages
were not very different; the way of life, the methods of
cultivation, very much the same. The colonists—for such

they had now become—brought their families from Scandinavia, but also it is certain that they established human and natural relations with the expropriated English. The blood-stream of these vigorous individualists, proud and successful men of the sword, mingled henceforward in the Island race. A vivifying, potent, lasting and resurgent quality was added to the breed. As modern steel is hardened by the alloy of special metals in comparatively small quantities, this strong strain of individualism, based upon land-ownership, was afterwards to play a persistent part, not only in the blood but in the politics of England. When in the reign of Henry II, after much disorder, great laws were made and royal courts of justice were opened descendants of these hardy farmers were found in a state of high assertiveness. The tribulations of another three hundred years had not destroyed their original firmness of character nor their deep attachment to the conquered soil. All through English history this strain continues to play a gleaming part.

We shall see presently the equitable, deferential terms which even after their final victory the Anglo-Saxon monarchs proffered to the districts settled by the Danes, known as the Danelaw. It remained only for conversion to Christianity to mingle these races inextricably in the soul and body of a nation. These considerations may aptly fill the five years' breathing space which Alfred had gained by courageous fighting and politic Danegeld. In this interval Halfdene, the Viking king, departed from the scene. The tortured, plundered Church requited his atrocities by declaring that God punished him in the long run by madness and a smell which made his presence unendurable to his fellows.

*   *   *

Alfred's dear-bought truce was over. Guthrum, the new war-leader of the mobile and martial part of the heathen army, had formed a large design for the subjugation of Wessex. He operated by sea and land, and proceeded to attack Alfred's kingdom by raid and storm from every quarter. The prudent King sought peace and offered an indemnity. The Danes took the gold, and "swore upon the Holy Ring" they would depart and keep a faithful peace. With a treachery to which all adjectives are unequal they suddenly darted away and seized Exeter. Alfred mounting his infantry, followed after, but arrived too late. But let all heathen beware of breaking oaths! A frightful tempest smote the sea army. They were smitten by the elements, which in those days were believed to be personally directed by the Almighty. A hundred and twenty ships were sunk, and upwards of five thousand of these perjured marauders perished as they deserved. Thus the whole careful plan fell to pieces and Alfred found his enemies in the summer of 877 in the mood for a new peace. They swore it with oaths of still more compliant solemnity, and they kept it for about five months.

Then in January 878 occurred the most surprising reversal of Alfred's fortunes. It was Twelfth Night, and the Saxons, who in these days of torment refreshed and fortified themselves by celebrating the feasts of the Church, were off their guard, engaged in pious exercises, or perhaps even drunk. Down swept the ravaging foe. The whole army of Wessex, sole guarantee of England south of the Thames, was dashed into confusion. Many were killed. The most part stole away to their houses. A strong contingent fled overseas. Only a handful of officers and personal attendants hid themselves with Alfred in the marshes and forests. This was the darkest hour of Alfred's fortunes.

Twelfth Night, an ancient festival called Epiphany, is held in the evening of the twelfth day after Christmas.

This is the moment when those gleaming toys of history were fashioned for the children of every age. We see the warrior-king disguised as a minstrel harping in the Danish camps. We see him acting as a kitchen-boy to a Saxon housewife. The celebrated story of Alfred and the Cakes first appears in a late edition of Bishop Asser's Life. It runs: "It happened one day that the countrywoman, who was the wife of the cowherd with whom King Alfred was staying, was going to bake bread, and the King was sitting by the fireside making ready his bow and arrows and other weapons. A moment came when the woman saw that her bread was burning; she rushed up and removed it from the fire, upbraiding the undaunted King

Bishop Asser was a Welsh monk, a companion of Alfred who wrote an account of the King's life. All writing in those days was in Latin and often in a conventional verse form.

with these words (recorded, strangely, in the original in Latin hexameters): 'Alack, man, why have you not turned over the bread when you see that it is burning, especially as you so much like eating it hot.' The misguided woman little thought that she was talking to King Alfred, who had fought so vigorously against the heathens and won so many victories over them." Low were the fortunes of the once ruthless English.

The leaders of the Danish army felt sure at this time that mastery was in their hands. To the people of Wessex it seemed that all was over. Their forces were dispersed, the country overrun; their King, if alive, was a fugitive in hiding. It is the supreme proof of Alfred's quality that he was able in such a plight to exercise his full authority and keep contact with his subjects.

Towards the end of Lent the Danes suffered an unexpected misfortune. The crews of twenty-three ships, after committing many atrocities in Wales, sailed to Devon and marched to the attack of one of Alfred's strongholds on Exmoor. Eight hundred Danes were killed and the spoils of the victory included an enchanted banner called the Raven, of which it was said that the three daughters of Ragnar Lodbrok had woven it in a single day, and that "in every battle in which that banner went before them the raven in the middle of the design seemed to flutter as though it were alive if they were going to have the victory." On this occasion it did not flutter, but hung listlessly in its silken folds. The event proved that it was impossible for the Danes to win under these conditions.

Ragnar was a semi-legendary Norse Viking supposed to have invaded England about 800.

Alfred, cheered by this news and striving to take the field again, continued a brigand warfare against the enemy while sending his messengers to summon the "fyrd," or local militia, for the end of May. There was a general response; the King was loved and admired. The news that he was alive and active caused widespread joy. All the fighting men came back. After all, the country was in peril of subjugation, the King was a hero, and they could always go home again.

The Danes still lay upon their plunder. Alfred advanced and on the bare downs was fought the largest and culminating battle of Alfred's wars. All was staked. All hung in the scales of fate. On both sides the warriors dismounted; the horses were sent to the rear. The shield-walls were formed, the masses clashed against each other, and for hours they fought with sword and axe. But the heathen had lost the favour of God through their violated oath, and eventually from this or other causes they fled from the cruel and clanging field. This time Alfred's pursuit was fruitful. Guthrum, king of the Viking army, so lately master of the one unconquered English kingdom, found himself penned in his camp. They offered to give without return as many hostages as Alfred should care to pick and to depart forthwith.

But Alfred had had longer ends in view. It is strange that he should have wished to convert these savage foes. Baptism as a penalty of defeat might lose its spiritual quality. The workings of the spirit are mysterious, but we must still wonder how the hearts of these hard-bitten swordsmen and pirates could be changed in a single day. Indeed these mass conversions had become almost a matter of form for defeated Viking armies. But Alfred meant to make a lasting peace with Guthrum. He had him and his army in his power. He could have starved them into surrender and slaughtered them to a man. He wished instead to divide the land with them, and that the two races, in spite of fearful injuries given and received, should dwell together in amity. He received Guthrum with thirty buccaneers in his camp. He stood godfather to Guthrum; he raised him from the font; he presented him and his warriors with costly gifts; he called him his son.

This sublime power to rise above the whole force of circumstances, to remain unbiased by the extremes of victory or defeat, to persevere in the teeth of disaster, to greet returning fortune with a cool eye, to have faith in men, after repeated betrayals, raises Alfred far above the turmoil of barbaric wars to his pinnacle of deathless glory.

*   *   *

Fourteen years intervened between the victory of Ethandun and any serious Danish attack. In spite of much

The Viking ships sail from Denmark to raid and pillage Saxon England. Alfred first meets and defeats the "Great Heathen Army" at Ashdown but he is later forced to make a heavy payment of "Danegeld" to buy a period of peace in which to gather his forces. The Danes break the truce and raid Alfred's army on Twelfth

Night, dispersing it and casting Alfred into exile. He wanders through the Danish camp disguised as a minstrel, burns the famous cakes, and finally regains the field at the Battle of Ethandun. Guthrum, the new Danish leader, is defeated but Alfred pardons him, baptizes him and thus brings a lasting peace to the land.

uneasiness and disturbance, by the standards of those days there was peace. Alfred worked ceaselessly to strengthen his realm.

The first result of this new unity was the recovery of London in 886. London had long been the emporium of Christian England. Ancient Rome had seen in this bridgehead of the Thames, at the convergence of all the roads and sea routes, the greatest commercial and military centre in the Island. Now the City was set on the road to becoming the national capital.

King Alfred's main effort was to restore the defences and raise the efficiency of the West Saxon force. The modesty of his reforms shows us the enormous difficulties which he had to overcome, and proves that even in that time of mortal peril it was almost impossible to keep the English under arms. He saw too the vision of English sea-power. To be safe in an island it was necessary to command the sea. He made great departures in ship design, and hoped to beat the Viking numbers by fewer ships of much larger size. These conclusions have only recently become antiquated. The beginning of the English Navy must always be linked with King Alfred.

King Alfred's Book of Laws, or Dooms, attempted to blend the Mosaic code with Christian principles and old Germanic customs. He inverted the Golden Rule. Instead of "Do unto others as you would that they should do unto you," he adopted the less ambitious principle, "What ye will that other men should *not* do to you, that do ye not to other men," with the comment, "By bearing this precept in mind a judge can do justice to all men; he needs no other law-books. Let him think of himself as the plaintiff, and consider what judgment would satisfy him." The King, in his preamble, explained modestly that "I have not dared to presume to set down in writing many laws of my own, for I cannot tell what will meet with the approval of our successors." The Laws of Alfred, continually amplified by his successors, grew into the Common Law.

The Saxon Chronicle was the first official history of England to be compiled from existing oral and written records.

Lastly in this survey comes Alfred's study of history. He it was who set on foot the compiling of the *Saxon Chronicle*. The fact that the early entries are fragmentary gives confidence that the compilers did not draw on their imagination. From King Alfred's time they are exact, often abundant, and sometimes written with historic grasp and eloquence.

We discern across the centuries a commanding and versatile intelligence, wielding with equal force the sword of war and of justice; using in defence arms and policy; cherishing religion, learning, and art in the midst of adversity and danger; welding together a nation, and seeking always across the feuds and hatreds of the age a peace which would smile upon the land.

In grim times the figure of the great Alfred was a beacon-light, the bright symbol of Saxon achievement, the hero of the race. The ruler who had taught them courage and self-reliance in the eternal Danish wars, who had sustained them with his national and religious faith, who had given them laws and good governance and chronicled their heroic deeds, was celebrated in legend and song as Alfred the Great.

One final war awaited Alfred. Guthrum died in 891, and the pact which he had sworn with Alfred, and loosely kept, ended. Suddenly in the autumn of 892 a hostile armada of two hundred and fifty ships appeared carrying "the Great Heathen Army." This immense concerted assault confronted Alfred with his third struggle for life. The English, as we may call them—for the Mercians and Saxons stood together—had secured fourteen years of unquiet peace in which to develop their defences. There had been a re-gathering of wealth and food; there was a settled administration, and the allegiance of all was given to King Alfred. Unlike Charlemagne, he had a valiant son. At twenty-two Edward could lead his father's armies to the field. The Mercians also had produced an Ethelred, who was a fit companion to the West Saxon prince. The King, in ill-health, is not often seen in this phase at the head of armies; we have glimpses of him, but the great episodes of the war were centred, as they should be, upon the young leaders.

The English beat the Vikings in this third war. The Danes had fortified themselves at Benfleet, on the Thames

The seat of power of the Danish settlers in England was the district of Mercia.

Charlemagne, 742–814, a great King of the French, or Franks as they were then called, was also Emperor of the Romans.

below London. This the princes now assaulted. It had very rarely been possible in these wars to storm a well-fortified place; but Alfred's son and his son-in-law with a strong army from London fell upon Benfleet and "put the army to flight, stormed the fort, and took all that there was within, goods as well as women and children, and brought all to London. And all the ships they either broke in pieces or burnt or brought to London or Rochester." Such are the words of the *Saxon Chronicle*. In the captured stronghold the victors found Haesten's wife and his two sons. These were precious hostages, and King Alfred was much criticised at the time, and also later, because he restored

Haesten was the Viking leader in Britain at this time.

them to Haesten. He sent back his wife on broad grounds of humanity. As for the two sons, they had been baptised; he was godfather to one of them, and Ethelred of Mercia to the other. They were therefore Christian brethren, and the King protected them from the consequences of their father's wrongful war. The ninth century found it very hard to understand this behaviour when the kingdom was fighting desperately against brutal marauders, but that is one of the reasons why in the after-time the King is called "Alfred the Great." The war went on, but so far as the records show Haesten never fought again. It may be that mercy and chivalry were not in vain.

Alfred had well defended the Island home. He had by policy and arms preserved the Christian civilisation in England. He had built up the strength of that mighty South which has ever since sustained much of the weight of Britain, and later of her Empire. He had liberated London, and happily he left behind him descendants who, for several generations, carried his work forward with valour

A.D. *901* and success.

KING HAROLD

1022-1066

WILLIAM the Conqueror

1027-1087

Rollo was a Norwegian Viking who, in 912, had conquered the large province of Normandy.

ONE MORNING Duke Robert of Normandy, the fourth descendant of Rollo, was riding towards his capital town, Falaise, when he saw Arlette, daughter of a tanner, washing linen in a stream. His love was instantly fired. He carried her to his castle, and, although already married to a lady of quality, lived with her for the rest of his days. To this romantic but irregular union there was born in 1027 a son, William, afterwards famous.

Duke Robert died when William was only seven, and in those harsh times a minor's hold upon his inheritance was precarious. The great nobles who were his guardians came one by one to violent ends, and rival ambitions stirred throughout Normandy. Was the grandson of a tanner to be the liege lord of the many warrior families?

It was the declared policy of the King of France to recognise and preserve the minor upon the ducal throne. He became William's feudal guardian and overlord. But for this the boy could hardly have survived. In 1047, when he was twenty, a formidable conspiracy was organised against him, and at the outset of the revolt he narrowly missed destruction. William was hunting in the heart of the disaffected country. His seizure was planned, but his

Most noblemen in these days had a "fool," or court jester, to amuse them.

fool broke in upon him with a timely warning to fly for his life. By daybreak he had ridden forty miles, and was for the moment safe in loyal Falaise. Knowing that his own strength could not suffice, he rode on ceaselessly to appeal for help to his overlord, the King of France. This was not denied. King Henry took the field. William gathered together his loyal barons and retainers. At the Battle of Val-és-Dunes, fought entirely on both sides by cavalry, the rebels were routed, and thenceforward, for the first time, William's position as Duke of Normandy was secure.

The sense of affinity to the liege lord at every stage in the hierarchy, the association of the land with fighting power, the acceptance of the Papal authority in spiritual matters, united the steel-clad knights and nobles over an ever-widening area of Europe. To the full acceptance of the universal Christian Church was added the conception of a warrior aristocracy, animated by ideas of chivalry, and knit together in a system of military service based upon the holding of land.

In no part of the feudal world was the fighting quality of the new organisation carried to a higher pitch than among the Normans. William was a master of war, and thereby gave his small duchy some of the prestige which England had enjoyed thirty years before under the firm and clear-sighted government of Canute. He and his knights now looked out upon the world with fearless and adventurous eyes. Good reasons for gazing across the Channel were added to the natural ambitions of warlike men.

Canute had been an "emperor" like Charlemagne over a northern empire which included Denmark, Norway, and England from 1017 to 1035.

Fate played startlingly into the hands of the Norman Duke. On some visit of inspection, probably in 1064, Harold was driven by the winds on to the French coast. A friendship sprang up between William and Harold. Politics apart, they liked each other well. We see them, falcon on wrist, in sport; Harold taking the field with William against the Bretons, or rendering skilful service in hazardous broils. He was honoured and knighted by William. But the Duke looked forward to his future succession to the English crown. Here indeed was the prize to be won. Harold had one small streak of royal blood on his mother's side; but William, through his father, had a more pointed or at least less cloudy claim to the Island throne. This claim he was resolved to assert. He saw the power which Harold wielded under King Edward the Confessor, and how easily he might convert it into sovereignty if he happened to be on the spot when the Confessor died. He invited Harold to make a pact with him whereby he himself should become King of England, and Harold Earl of the whole splendid province of Wessex, being assured thereof and linked to the King by marriage with William's daughter.

Harold was the son of the most trusted counsellor of King Edward the Confessor.

The people of Brittany were called Bretons.

All this story is told with irresistible charm in the tapestry chronicle of the reign commonly attributed to William's wife, Queen Matilda, but actually designed by English artists under the guidance of his half-brother, Odo, Bishop of Bayeux. It is probable that Harold swore a solemn oath to William to renounce all rights or designs upon the English crown, and it is likely that if he had not done so he might never have seen either crown or England again.

The feudal significance of this oath making Harold William's man was enhanced by a trick novel to those times, yet adapted to their mentality. Under the altar or table upon which Harold swore there was concealed a sacred relic, said by some later writers to have been some of the bones of St. Edmund. An oath thus reinforced had a triple sanctity, well recognised throughout Christendom. It was a super-oath; and the obligation, although taken unbeknown, was none the less binding upon Harold. Nevertheless it cannot be said that the bargain between the two men was unreasonable, and Harold probably at the time saw good prospects in it for himself.

St. Edmund, King of East Anglia, was killed by the Danes, 870.

By this time William had consolidated his position at home. He had destroyed the revolting armies of his rivals and ambitious relations. He had forced the powers in Paris who had protected his youth to respect his manhood.

Meanwhile Harold, liberated, was conducting the government of England with genuine acceptance and increasing success. At length, in January 1066, Edward the Confessor died, absolved, we trust, from such worldly sins as he had been tempted to commit. With his dying breath, in spite of his alleged promise to William, he is supposed to have commended Harold, his young, valiant counsellor and guide, as the best choice for the crown which the Witan, or Council, could make. At any rate, Harold, at the beginning of the fateful year 1066, was blithely accepted by London, the Midlands, and the South, and crowned King with all solemnity in Westminster Abbey.

This event opened again the gates of war. Every aspiring thane who heard the news of Harold's elevation was conscious of an affront, and also of the wide ranges open to ability and the sword. Moreover, the entire structure of the feudal world rested upon the sanctity of oaths. Against the breakers of oaths the censures both of chivalry and the Church were combined with blasting force. Rome therefore could not recognise Harold as King.

At this very moment the Almighty, reaching down from His heavenly sphere, made an ambiguous gesture. The tailed comet or "hairy star" which appeared at the time

of Harold's coronation is now identified by astronomers
as Halley's Comet, which had previously heralded the
Nativity of Our Lord; and it is evident that this example
of divine economy in the movements for mundane purposes of celestial bodies might have been turned by deft
interpretation to Harold's advantage. But the conquerors
have told the tale, and in their eyes this portent conveyed
to men the approaching downfall of a sacrilegious upstart.

Two rival projects of invasion were speedily prepared.
The first was from Scandinavia. An expedition was already
being organised when Tostig, Harold's exiled and revenge-
ful half-brother, arrived with full accounts of the crisis in
the Island and of the weak state of the defences. King
Harold Hardrada set forth to conquer the English crown.   *Harold Hardrada, "the Stern,"*
With Tostig he wended towards the north-east coast of   *was King of Norway, 1046–1066.*
England with a large fleet and army in the late summer
of 1066.

Harold of England was thus faced with a double invasion from the north-east and from the south. In September 1066 he heard that a Norwegian fleet, with Hardrada
and Tostig on board, had beaten the local levies and en-
camped near York. He now showed the fighting qualities
he possessed. The news reached him in London, where
he was waiting to see which invasion would strike him
first, and where. At the head of his household troops he
hastened northwards up the Roman road to York, calling out the local levies as he went. His rapidity of movement took the Northern invaders completely by surprise.
Within five days Harold reached York, and the same day
marched to confront the Norwegian army ten miles from
the city.

The battle began. The Englishmen charged, but at
first the Norsemen though without their armour, kept their
battle array. After a while, deceived by what proved to be
a feint, the common ruse of those days, they opened up
their shield rampart and advanced from all sides. This was
the moment for which Harold had waited. The greatest
crash of weapons arose. Hardrada was hit by an arrow
in the throat, and Tostig, assuming the command, took his
stand by the banner "Landravager." In this pause Harold

offered his brother peace, and also quarter to all Norsemen who were still alive; but "the Norsemen called out
all of them together that they would rather fall, one across
the other, than accept of quarter from the Englishmen."
Harold's valiant house-carls, themselves of Viking blood,
charged home, and with a war shout the battle began
again. The victorious Harold buried Hardrada in the
seven feet of English earth he had scornfully promised him,
but he spared his son Olaf and let him go in peace with
his surviving adherents. Tostig paid for his restless malice
with his life. Though the Battle of Stamford Bridge has
been overshadowed by Hastings it has a claim to be regarded as one of the decisive contests of English history.
Never again was a Scandinavian army able seriously to
threaten the power of an English king or the unity of the
realm.

At the moment of victory news reached the King from
the South that "William the Bastard" had landed at
Pevensey.

*   *   *

William the Conqueror's invasion of England was
planned like a business enterprise. The resources of Normandy were obviously unequal to the task; but the idea of
seizing and dividing England commended itself to the martial nobility of many lands. The shares in this enterprise
were represented by knights or ships, and it was plainly
engaged that the lands of the slaughtered English would
be divided in proportion to the contributions, subject of
course to a bonus for good work in the field. During the
summer of 1066 this great gathering of audacious buccaneers, land-hungry, war-hungry, assembled in a merry company at the mouth of the Somme. Ships had been built
in all the French ports from the spring onwards, and by
the beginning of August nearly seven hundred vessels and
about seven thousand men, of whom the majority were
persons of rank and quality, were ready to follow the renowned Duke and share the lands and wealth of England.

But the winds were contrary. For six whole weeks there
was no day when the south wind blew. At length extreme

measures had to be taken with the weather. The bones of
St. Edmund were brought from the church of St. Valery
and carried with military and religious pomp along the
seashore. This proved effective, for the very next day the
wind changed. William gave the signal. The whole fleet
put to sea, with all their stores, weapons, coats of mail
and great numbers of horses.

On September 28 the fleet came safely to anchor in
Pevensey Bay. William landed, as the tale goes, and fell
flat on his face as he stepped out of the boat. "See," he
said, turning the omen into a favourable channel, "I have
taken England with both my hands."

Meanwhile Harold and his house-carls, sadly depleted
by the slaughter of Stamford Bridge, jingled down Watling
Street on their ponies, marching night and day to London.
They covered the two hundred miles in seven days. In
London the King gathered all the forces he could, and
remaining only five days in the city marched out towards
Pevensey, and took up his position upon the slope of a
hill which barred the direct march upon the capital.

King Harold had great confidence in his redoubtable
axe-men, and it was in good heart that he formed his
shield-wall on the morning of October 14. At the first
streak of dawn William set out from his camp at Pevensey,
resolved to put all to the test; and Harold, eight miles
away, awaited him in resolute array.

The autumn afternoon was far spent before any result
had been achieved, and it was then that William adopted
the time-honoured ruse of a feigned retreat. The house-
carls around Harold preserved their discipline and kept
their ranks, but the sense of relief to the less trained forces
after these hours of combat was such that seeing their
enemy in flight proved irresistible. They surged forward
on the impulse of victory, and when half-way down the
hill were savagely slaughtered by William's horsemen.
There remained, as the dusk grew, only the valiant body-
guard who fought round the King and his standard. His
brothers Gyrth and Leofwine, had already been killed.
William now directed his archers to shoot high into the
air, so that the arrows would fall behind the shield-wall,

WILLIAM, DUKE OF NORMANDY

HAROLD, KING OF ENGLAND

PEVENSEY •

• HASTINGS

ST. VALERY

William prepares for the invasion in Normandy. Harold reigns in England and marches to meet William. Westminster Abbey, not yet half-finished, is in the background. Below, the peasants ploughing are symbolic of the constancy of life in Saxon England. The "hairy star" (Halley's Comet) is a bad omen for Harold, who

dies at the battle of Hastings. Here he is shown upside down, shot in the eye by an arrow. Bloody turmoil ends in the conquest of the countryside by William, holding his favorite weapon, the mace. Norman forts and castles prevail, but the Saxon peasant continues as before.

and one of these pierced Harold in the right eye, inflicting a mortal wound. He fell at the foot of the royal standard, unconquerable except by death, which does not count in honour. The hard-fought battle was now decided and William, who had fought in the foremost ranks and had three horses killed under him, could claim the victory.

The dead king's naked body, wrapped only in a robe of purple, was hidden among the rocks of the bay. His mother in vain offered the weight of the body in gold for permission to bury him in holy ground. The Norman Duke's answer was that Harold would be more fittingly laid upon the Saxon shore which he had given his life to defend. Although here the English once again accepted conquest and bowed in a new destiny, yet ever must the name of Harold be honoured in the Island for which he and his famous house-carls fought indomitably to the end.

William was a prime exponent of the doctrine, so well known in this civilised age as "frightfulness"—of mass terorism through the spectacle of bloody and merciless examples.

When William arrived near London he marched round the city by a circuitous route, isolating it by a belt of cruel desolation until the Saxon notables and clergy came meekly to his tent to offer him the crown. On Christmas Day Aldred, Archbishop of York, crowned him King of England at Westminster. He rapidly established his power over all England south of the Humber. Within two years of the conquest Duchess Matilda, who ruled Normandy in William's absence, came across the sea to her coronation at Westminster on Whit Sunday 1068, and later in the year a son, Henry, symbol and portent of dynastic stability, was born on English soil.

For at least twenty years after the invasion the Normans were an army camped in a hostile country, holding the population down by castles at key points. The Saxon resistance died hard. Legends and chroniclers have painted for us the last stand of Hereward the Wake in the broad wastes of the fens round Ely. Not until five years after Hastings in 1071 was Hereward put down. The building of Ely Castle symbolised the end.

Churchill wrote these lines early in 1939 before Hitler started the Second World War by invading Poland.

Westminster, formerly a city now part of London, is noted for the abbey around which it grew up and for the houses of Parliament and government buildings.

The name Whit Sunday (white days-week) refers to the white garments worn by candidates for baptism. It is a church festival held on the seventh Sunday after Easter celebrating the feast of Pentecost.

Hereward the Wake was a noted English outlaw and patriot. Many legends sprang up later around his name.

Norman castles guarded the towns, Norman lords held the land, and Norman churches protected men's souls. All England had a master, the conquest was complete, and the work of reconstruction began.

Woe to the conquered! Here were the Normans entrenched on English soil, masters of the land and the fullness thereof. Everywhere castles arose. These were not at first the massive stone structures of a later century; they were simply fortified military posts consisting of an earthen rampart and a stockade, and a central keep made of logs. From these strongpoints horsemen sallied forth to rule and exploit the neighbourhood; above them all, at the summit, sat William, active and ruthless, delighting in his work, requiring punctual service from his adherents, and paying good spoil to all who did their duty.

Meanwhile, years passed. Queen Matilda was a capable regent at Rouen, but plagued by the turbulence of her sons. The eldest, Robert, a Crusading knight, reckless and spendthrift, with his father's love of fighting and adventure but without his ruthless genius or solid practical aims, resented William's persistent hold on life and impatiently claimed his Norman inheritance. Many a time the father was called across the Channel to chastise rebellious towns and forestall the conspiracies of his son with the French Court. Robert, driven from his father's lands, found refuge in King Philip's castle. William marched implacably upon him. Beneath the walls two men, visor down, met in single combat, father and son. Robert wounded his father in the hand and unhorsed him, and would indeed have killed him but for a timely rescue by an Englishman, one Tokig of Wallingford, who remounted the overthrown conqueror. Both were sobered by this chance encounter, and for a time there was reconciliation.

Matilda died, and with increasing years William became fiercer in mood. Stung to fury by the forays of the French, he crossed the frontier, spreading fire and ruin till he reached the gates of Mantes. His Normans surprised the town, and amid the horrors of the sack fire broke out. As William rode through the streets his horse stumbled among the burning ashes and he was thrown against the pommel of the saddle. He was carried in agony to the priory of St. Gervase at Rouen. There, high above the town, he lay, through the summer heat of 1087, fighting his grievous injury. When death drew near his younger sons William and Henry came to him. William, whose one virtue had been filial fidelity, was named to succeed the Conqueror in England. The graceless Robert would rule in Normandy at last. For the youngest, Henry, there was nothing but five thousand pounds of silver, and the prophecy that he would one day reign over a united Anglo-Norman nation. This proved no empty blessing.

The Norman achievement in England was not merely military in character. Although knight-service governed the holding of property and produced a new aristocracy, much was preserved of Saxon England. The whole system of Saxon local government, also of immense usefulness for the future—the counties, the sheriffs, and the courts—survived, and through this the King maintained his widespread contacts with the country. Thus in the future government of England both Norman and Saxon institutions were unconsciously but profoundly blended.

The essence of Norman feudalism was that the land remained under the lord, whatever the man might do. Thus the landed pyramid rose up tier by tier to the King, until every acre in the country could be registered as held of somebody by some form of service. The survival of the hundred, the county court and the sheriff makes the great difference between English and Continental feudalism.

The "hundred" was an ancient territorial unit less than a shire or county and usually greater than a parish or town. The origin of the name is obscure but is supposed to be a grouping of 100 families for defence or government. The land area varied greatly in different regions.

In the Norman settlement lay the germ of a constitutional opposition, with the effect if not the design of controlling the Government, not breaking it up. The little provinces of England, with the King's officers at the head of each, gave William exactly the balance of power he needed for all purposes of law and finance, but were at the same time incapable of rebelling as units.

The Conquest was the supreme achievement of the Norman race. It linked the history of England anew to Europe, and prevented for ever a drift into the narrower orbit of a Scandinavian empire. Henceforward English history marched with that of races and lands south of the Channel.

HENRY PLANTAGENET

1133-1189

THOMAS BECKET

1118-1170

ELEANOR OF AQUITAINE

KING STEPHEN

"FAIR ROSAMOND"

THE CONSTITUTIONS OF CLARENDON

MURDER IN THE CATHEDRAL

THE FOUR EAGLETS

Robert, Earl of Gloucester,
an illegitimate son of Henry I,
had been a possible successor
to the childless Stephen
who was King at this time.

In 1147 ROBERT OF GLOUCESTER died and Henry Plantagenet was born to empire. He carried into English history the emblem of his house, the broom, the *Planta Genesta,* which later generations were to make the name of this great dynasty, the Plantagenets. He embodied all their ability, all their energy, and not a little of that passionate, ruthless ferocity which, it was whispered, came to the house of Anjou from no mortal source, but from a union with Satan himself.

His father was a French noble,
Geoffrey of Anjou, and his mother
Matilda was Stephen's sister.

In 1150 Henry was invested by his parents as Duke of Normandy. The next year his father's death made him also Count of Anjou, Touraine, and Maine. In his high feudal capacity Henry repaired to Paris to render homage to his lord the King of France.

King Louis VII was a French Edward the Confessor; he practised with faithful simplicity the law of Christ. All his days were spent in devotion, and his nights in vigil or penance. When he left his own chapel he would delay the whole Court by waiting till the humblest person present had preceded him. These pious and exemplary habits did not endear him to his queen. Eleanor of Aquitaine was in her own right a reigning princess, with the warmth of the South in her veins. She had already complained that she had "married a monk and not a king" when this square-shouldered, ruddy youth, with his "countenance of fire," sprightly talk, and overflowing energy, suddenly presented himself before her husband as his most splendid vassal. Eleanor did not waste words in coming to a decision. The Papacy bowed to strong will in the high feudal chiefs, and Eleanor obtained a divorce from Louis VII in

There were many marriage laws
subject to many interpretations
concerning consanguinity, or
blood relationships.

1152 on the nominal grounds of consanguinity. But what staggered the French Court and opened the eyes of its prayerful King was the sudden marriage of Eleanor to Henry two months later. Thus half of France passed out of royal control into the hands of Henry. Rarely have passion and policy flowed so buoyantly together. The marriage was one of the most brilliant political strokes of the age. Henry afterwards admitted his designs, and accepted the admiration of Europe for their audacity. He was nineteen and she was probably thirty; and uniting their im-

32

mense domains, they made common cause against all comers. To Louis VII were vouchsafed the consolations of the spirit; but even these were jarred upon by the problems of government.

War in all quarters lay before the royal pair. Everywhere men shook their heads over this concentration of power, this spectacle of so many races and states, sundered from each other by long feuds or divergent interests, now suddenly flung together by the hot blood of a love intrigue. From all sides the potentates confronted the upstart.

A month after the marriage these foes converged upon Normandy. But the youthful Duke Henry beat them back, ruptured and broken. The Norman army proved once again its fighting quality. Before he was twenty Henry turned to England. It was a valiant figure that landed in January 1153, and from all over England, distracted by civil wars, hearts and eyes turned towards him. Merlin had prophesied a deliverer: had he not in his veins blood that ran back to William the Conqueror? A wild surge of hope greeted him from the tormented Islanders.

Merlin was a half-legendary bard of the sixth century, a magician and a companion and counsellor to King Arthur. It was Merlin who instituted the famous Round Table. His mistress Vivien, the "Lady of the Lake," is said to have left him spellbound in the tangled branches of a thornbush, where he still sleeps though his prophecies continue to be heard even these many hundred years later.

There followed battles: Malmesbury, where the sleet, especially directed by Almighty God, beat upon the faces of his foes; Wallingford, where King Stephen by divine interposition fell three times from his horse before going into action. Glamour, terror, success, attended this youthful, puissant warrior, who had not only his sword, but his title-deeds. And when a year later Stephen died he was acclaimed and crowned King of England with more general hope and rejoicing than had ever uplifted any monarch in England since the days of Alfred the Great.

The accession of Henry II began one of the most pregnant and decisive reigns in English history. The new sovereign ruled an empire, and, as his subjects boasted, his warrant ran "from the Arctic Ocean to the Pyrenees." England to him was but one—the most solid though perhaps the least attractive—of his provinces. But he gave to England that effectual element of external control which was indispensable to the growth of national unity. He was accepted by English and Norman as the ruler of both races and the whole country. The memories of Hastings were confounded in his person, and after the hideous anarchy of civil war and robber barons all due attention was paid to his commands. Thus, though a Frenchman, with foreign speech and foreign modes, he shaped our country in a fashion of which the outline remains to the present day.

After a hundred years of being the encampment of an invading army and the battleground of its quarrelsome officers and their descendants England became finally and for all time a coherent kingdom, based upon Christianity and upon that Latin civilisation which recalled the message of ancient Rome. Henry Plantagenet first brought England, Scotland, and Ireland into a certain common relationship; he re-established the system of royal government which his grandfather, Henry I, had prematurely erected. He relaid the foundations of a central power, based upon the exchequer and the judiciary, which was ultimately to supersede the feudal system of William the Conqueror. The King gathered up and cherished the Anglo-Saxon tradition of self-government under royal command in shire and borough; he developed and made permanent "assizes" as they survive today. It is to him we owe the enduring fact that the English-speaking race all over the world is governed by the English Common Law rather than by the Roman.

In these early days assizes were juries sitting together for the trial of a cause. The term later signified courts, circuits, judicial assemblies.

A vivid picture is painted of this gifted and, for a while enviable man; square, thick-set, bull-necked, with powerful arms and coarse, rough hands; his legs bandy

England
Woodstock
Malmesbury Wallingford
Canterbury

English Channel

Normandy

Brittany   Maine
Anjou   Touraine

Aquitaine

Gascony

Pyrenees

from endless riding; a large, round head and closely cropped red hair; a freckled face; a voice harsh and cracked. Intense love of the chase; other loves, which the Church deplored and Queen Eleanor resented; frugality in food and dress; days entirely concerned with public business; travel unceasing; moods various. It was said that he was always gentle and calm in times of urgent peril, but became bad-tempered and capricious when the pressure relaxed. He journeyed hotfoot around his many dominions, arriving unexpectedly in England when he was thought to be in the South of France. He carried with him in his tours of each province wains loaded with ponderous rolls which represented the office files of to-day. His Court and train gasped and panted behind him. Sometimes, when he had appointed an early start, he was sleeping till noon, with all the wagons and pack-horses awaiting him fully laden. Sometimes he would be off hours before the time he had fixed, leaving everyone to catch up as best they could. Everything was stirred and moulded by him in England, as also in his other much greater estates, which he patrolled with tireless attention.

But this twelfth-century monarch, with his lusts and sports, his hates and his schemes, was no materialist; he was the Lord's Anointed, he commanded, with the Archbishop of Canterbury—"those two strong steers that drew the plough of England"—the whole allegiance of his subjects. The offices of religion, the fear of eternal damnation, the hope of even greater realms beyond the grave, accompanied him from hour to hour. At times he was smitten with remorse and engulfed in repentance. He drew all possible delights and satisfactions from this world and the next. He is portrayed to us in convulsions both of spiritual exaltation and abasement. This was no secluded monarch: the kings of those days were as accessible to all classes as a modern President of the United States. People broke in upon him at all hours with business, with tidings, with gossip, with visions, with complaints. Talk rang high in the King's presence and even to His Majesty's face among the nobles and courtiers.

Few mortals have led so full a life as Henry II or have

drunk so deeply of the cups of triumph and sorrow. In later life he fell out with Eleanor. When she was over fifty and he but forty-two he is said to have fallen in love with "Fair Rosamond," a damosel of high degree and transcendent beauty, and generations have enjoyed the romantic tragedy of Queen Eleanor penetrating the protecting maze at Woodstock by the clue of a silken thread and offering her hapless supplanter the hard choice between the dagger and the poisoned cup. Tiresome investigators have undermined this excellent tale, but it certainly should find its place in any history worthy of the name.

Woodstock, near Oxford, was a country residence of early English Kings. Later it was granted to the great Duke of Marlborough, Churchill's ancestor. On the property he built Blenheim Palace, where Sir Winston spent his youth and where he is now buried.

No episode opens to us a wider window upon the politics of the twelfth century in England than the quarrel of Henry II with his great subject and former friend, Thomas Becket, Archbishop of Canterbury. We have to realise the gravity of this conflict. The military State in feudal Christendom bowed to the Church in things spiritual; it never accepted the idea of the transference of secular power to priestly authority. But the Church, enriched continually by the bequests of hardy barons, anxious in the death agony about their life beyond the grave, became the greatest landlord and capitalist in the community. Rome used its ghostly arts upon the superstitions of almost all the actors in the drama. The power of the State was held in constant challenge by this potent interest. Questions of doctrine might well have been resolved, but how was the government of the country to be carried on under two conflicting powers, each possessed of immense claims upon limited national resources? This conflict was not confined to England. It was the root question of the European world, as it then existed.

Lanfranc was made Archbishop of Canterbury by William the Conqueror in 1070.

Under William the Conqueror schism had been avoided in England by tact and compromise. Under Lanfranc the Church worked with the Crown, and each power reinforced the other against the turbulent barons or the oppressed commonalty. But now a great personality stood at the summit of the religious hierarchy, Thomas Becket, who had been the King's friend. He had been his Chancellor. He had in both home and foreign affairs loyally served his master. He had re-organised the imposition of scutage, a tax that allowed money to commute personal service in arms and thus eventually pierced the feudal system to its core. He had played his part in the acquisition of Brittany. The King felt sure that in Becket he had his own man—no mere servant, but a faithful comrade and colleague in the common endeavour. It was by the King's direct influence and personal effort that Becket was elected Archbishop.

From that moment all his gifts and impulses ran in another channel. Something like the transformation which carried Henry V from a rollicking prince to the august hero-King overnight was now witnessed in Becket. His private life had always been both pious and correct. He had of course been immersed in political affairs; nor was it as a sombre figure behind the throne. But whereas hitherto as a courtier and a prince he had rivalled all in magnificence and pomp, taking his part in the vivid pageant of the times, he now sought by extreme austerities to gather around himself the fame and honour of a saint. Becket pursued the same methods and ambitions in the ecclesiastical as previously he had done in the political sphere; and in both he excelled. He now championed the Church against the Crown in every aspect of their innumerable interleaving functions. He clothed this aggressive process with those universal ideas of the Catholic Church and the Papal authority which far transcended the bounds of our Island, covering Europe and reaching out into the mysterious and the sublime. After a tour upon the Continent and a conclave with the religious dignitaries of France and Italy he returned to England imbued with the resolve to establish the independence of the Church hierarchy on the State as represented by the King. Thus he opened the conflict which the wise Lanfranc had throughout his life striven to avoid. At this time the mood in England was ripe for strife upon this issue.

In a loose and undefined way Saxon England had thought of the monarch as appointed by God, not only to rule the State, but to protect and guide the Church. Rome now began to make claims that the government of the Church ought to be in the hands of the clergy, under the

HENRY II

ELEANOR

THOMAS BECKET

Eleanor follows the silken thread in search of "Fair Rosamond" to offer her the choice between the dagger and the poisoned cup. Behind Henry is Becket, first as Henry's faithful minister and comrade, then as high churchman. The white space symbolizes the interval before Becket as Archbishop returns to Canterbury

Cathedral where he is murdered by Henry's four knights. Henry subjects himself in penance to public scourging by the monks. The end of Henry's life is tragically dominated by his sons, the "four eaglets," and Eleanor turns away from Henry, looking to the succession of her sons.

supervision of the Pope. According to this view, the King was a mere layman whose one religious function was obedience to the hierarchy. The Church was a body apart, with its own allegiance and its own laws.

The struggle between Henry II and Becket is confused by the technical details over which it was fought. There was however good reason why the quarrel should have been engaged upon incidents of administration rather than upon the main principles which were at stake. The Crown resented the claim of the Church to interfere in the State; but in the Middle Ages no king dared to challenge the Church outright, or, much as he might hope to limit its influence, thought of a decisive breach.

The Church in England, like the baronage, had gained greatly in power since the days of William the Conqueror and his faithful Archbishop Lanfranc. Henry schemed to regain what had been lost, and as the first step in 1162 appointed his trusted servant Becket to be Archbishop of Canterbury, believing he would thus secure the acquiescence of the Episcopacy. In fact he provided the Church with a leader of unequalled vigour and obstinacy. He ignored or missed the ominous signs of the change in Becket's attitude, and proceeded to his second step, the publication in 1164 of the Constitutions of Clarendon. In these Henry claimed, not without considerable truth, to be restating the customs of the kingdom as they had been before the anarchy of Stephen's reign. He sought to retrace thirty years and to annul the effects of Stephen's surrender. But Becket resisted. He regarded Stephen's yieldings as irrevocable gains by the Church. He refused to let them lapse. He declared that the Constitutions of Clarendon did not represent the relations between Church and Crown. When, in October 1164, he was summoned to appear before the Great Council and explain his conduct he haughtily denied the King's authority and placed himself under the protection of the Pope and God.

Thus he ruptured that unity which had hitherto been deemed vital in the English realm, and in fact declared war with ghostly weapons upon the King. Stiff in defiance, Becket took refuge on the Continent, where the same conflict was already distracting both Germany and Italy. The whole thought of the ruling classes in England was shaken by this grievous dispute. Only in 1170 was an apparent reconciliation brought about between him and the King. Each side appeared to waive its claims in principle. The King did not mention his rights and customs. The Archbishop was not called upon to give an oath. He was promised a safe return and full possession of his see.

Meanwhile in Becket's absence, Henry had resolved to secure the peaceful accession of his son, the young Henry, by having him crowned in his own lifetime. The ceremony had been performed by the Archbishop of York, assisted by a number of other clerics. This action was bitterly resented by Becket as an infringement of a cherished right of his see. After their agreement Henry supposed that bygones were to be bygones. But Becket had other views.

His welcome home after the years of exile was astonishing. At Canterbury the monks received him as an angel of God. "I am come to die among you," he said in his sermon, and again, "In this church there are martyrs, and God will soon increase their number." He made a triumphal progress through London, scattering alms to the beseeching and exalted people. Then hotfoot he proceeded to renew his excommunication of the clergy who had taken part in the crowning of young Henry. These unfortunate priests and prelates travelled in a bunch to the King, who was in Normandy. They told a tale not only of an ecclesiastical challenge, but of actual revolt and usurpation. They said that the Archbishop was ready "to tear the crown from the young King's head."

Henry Plantagenet, first of all his line, with all the fire of his nature, received these tidings when surrounded by his knights and nobles. He was transported with passion. "What a pack of fools and cowards," he cried, "I have nourished in my house, that not one of them will avenge me of this turbulent priest!" Four of the knights had heard the King's bitter words spoken in the full circle. They travelled fast to the coast. They crossed the Channel. They called for horses and rode to Canterbury. There on December 29, 1170, they found the Archbishop in the cathedral. The scene and the tragedy are famous. He confronted them with Cross and mitre, fearless and resolute in warlike action, a master of the histrionic arts. After haggard parleys they fell upon him, cut him down with their swords, and left him bleeding like Julius Caesar, with a score of wounds to cry for vengeance.

This tragedy was fatal to the King. The murder of one of the foremost of God's servants, like the breaking of a feudal oath, struck at the heart of the age. All England was filled with terror. They acclaimed the dead Archbishop as a martyr; and immediately it appeared that his relics healed incurable diseases, and robes that he had worn by their mere touch relieved minor ailments. Here indeed was a crime, vast and inexpiable. When Henry heard the appalling news he was prostrated with grief and fear. All the elaborate process of law which he had sought to set on foot against this rival power was brushed aside by a brutal, bloody act; and though he had never dreamed that such a deed would be done there were his own hot words, spoken before so many witnesses, to fasten on him, for that age at least, the guilt of murder, and, still worse, sacrilege.

The immediately following years were spent in trying to recover what he had lost by a great parade of atonement for his guilt. He made pilgrimages to the shrine of the murdered Archbishop. He subjected himself to public penances. On several anniversaries, stripped to the waist and kneeling humbly, he submitted to be scourged by the triumphant monks. Under this display of contrition and submission the King laboured perseveringly to regain the rights of State. By the Compromise of Avranches in 1172 he made his peace with the Papacy on comparatively easy terms. To many deep-delving historians it seems that in fact, though not in form, he had by the end of his life re-established the main principles of the Constitutions of Clarendon, which are after all in harmony with what the English nation or any virile and rational race would mean to have as their law. Certainly the Papacy supported him in his troubles with his sons. The knights, it is affirmed, regained their salvation in the holy wars. But Becket's sombre sacrifice had not been in vain.

It is a proof of the quality of the age that these fierce contentions, shaking the souls of men, should have been so rigorously and yet so evenly fought out. In modern conflicts and revolutions in some great states bishops and archbishops have been sent by droves to concentration camps, or pistolled in the nape of the neck in the well-warmed, brilliantly lighted corridor of a prison. What claim have we to vaunt a superior civilisation to Henry II's times? We are sunk in a barbarism all the deeper because it is tolerated by moral lethargy and covered with a veneer of scientific conveniences.

Churchill wrote this passage in 1938, obviously thinking of the Nazi crimes that were being committed by Hitler at the time.

*   *   *

Eighteen years of life lay before the King after Becket's death. In a sense, they were years of glory. Yet Henry knew well that his splendour was personal in origin, tenuous and transient in quality; and he had also deep clouding family sorrows. During these years he was confronted with no less than four rebellions by his sons. On each occasion they could count on the active support of the watchful King of France. Henry treated his ungrateful children with generosity, but he had no illusions. The royal chamber at Westminster at this time was adorned with paintings done at the King's command. One represented four eaglets preying upon the parent bird, the fourth one poised at the parent's neck, ready to pick out the eyes. "The four eaglets," the King is reported to have said, "are my four sons who cease not to persecute me even unto death. The youngest of them, whom I now embrace with so much affection will sometime in the end insult me more grievously and more dangerously than any of the others."

When he saw in the list of conspirators against him the name of his son John, upon whom his affection had strangely rested, he abandoned the struggle with life. "Let things go as they will," he gasped. "Shame, shame, on a conquered King." So saying, this hard, violent, brilliant and lonely man expired on July 6, 1189. The pious were taught to regard this melancholy end as the further chastisement of God upon the murderer of Thomas Becket. Such is the bitter taste of wordly power. Such are the correctives of glory.

RICHARD, Coeur de Lion

1157-1199

THE CHRISTIAN kingdom founded at Jerusalem after the First Crusade had stood precariously for a century. At length the rise of a great national leader of the Turks, or Saracens, united the Moslem power. In 1169 Saladin became Vizier of Egypt. Shortly afterwards he proclaimed himself Sultan. Soon his power was stretching out into Syria, encircling the Crusaders' principalities on the Levantine coast. In 1186 Saladin proclaimed a Holy War. He promised his warlike hordes booty and adventure in this world and bliss eternal in the next, and advanced upon Jerusalem. The Christian army of occupation, perhaps ten thousand strong, was caught at a disadvantage in the thirsty desert and cut to pieces by greatly superior numbers, and thereafter all Palestine and Syria, except Tyre, Antioch, and Tripoli, fell again into Moslem hands.

The First Crusade had ended with the capture of Jerusalem in 1099.

The shock of these events resounded throughout Europe. The Pope shared the general horror of the Christian West. His legates traversed the Courts enjoining peace among Christians and war against the infidel. The sovereigns of the three greatest nations of the West responded to the call, and an intense movement stirred the chivalry of England, France, and Germany.

In the midst of these surgings Henry II died in sorrow and disaster. He made no attempt to prescribe the succession, and it passed naturally to Richard. The new King affected little grief at the death of a father against whom he was in arms. He knelt beside his bier no longer than would have been necessary to recite the Lord's Prayer, and turned at once to the duties of his realm. In spite of many harsh qualities, men saw in him a magnanimity which has added lustre to his military renown. At the outset of his reign he gave an outstanding example. During his rebellion against his father he had pressed hard upon Henry II's rout at Le Mans in the very forefront of the cavalry without even wearing his mail. In the rearguard of the beaten army stood Henry's faithful warrior, William the Marshal. He confronted Richard and had him at his mercy. "Spare me!" cried Richard in his disadvantage; so the Marshal turned his lance against the prince's horse and killed it, saying with scorn, "I will not slay you. The

Devil may slay you." This was humiliation and insult worse than death. It was not therefore without anxiety that the Marshal and his friends awaited their treatment at the hands of the sovereign to whom their loyalties must now be transferred. But King Richard rose at once above the past. He spoke with dignity and detachment of the grim incident so fresh and smarting in his mind. He confirmed his father's true servant in all his offices and honours, and sent him to England to act in his name. He gave him in marriage the rich Crown heiress of Pembroke, and at a stroke the Marshal became one of the most powerful of English barons.

Richard, with all his characteristic virtues and faults cast in a heroic mould, is one of the most fascinating medieval figures. He has been described as the creature and embodiment of the age of chivalry. In those days the lion was much admired in heraldry, and more than one king sought to link himself with its repute. When Richard's contemporaries called him "Coeur de Lion" they paid a lasting compliment to the king of beasts. Little did the English people owe him for his services, and heavily did they pay for his adventures. He was in England only twice for a few short months in his ten years' reign; yet his memory has always stirred English hearts, and seems to present throughout the centuries the pattern of the fighting man. In all deeds of prowess as well as in large schemes of war Richard shone. He was tall and delicately shaped; strong in nerve and sinew, and most dexterous in arms. He rejoiced in personal combat, and regarded his opponents without malice as necessary agents in his fame. He loved war, not so much for the sake of glory or political ends, but as other men love science and poetry, for the excitement of the struggle and the glow of victory. By this his whole temperament was toned; and, united with the highest qualities of the military commander, love of war called forth all the powers of his mind and body.

Although a man of blood and violence, Richard was too impetuous to be either treacherous or habitually cruel. He was as ready to forgive as he was hasty to offend; he was open-handed and munificent to profusion; in war cir-

cumspect in design and skilful in execution; in politics a
child, lacking in subtlety and experience. His political alliances were formed upon his likes and dislikes; his political schemes had neither unity nor clearness of purpose.
The advantages gained for him by military genius were
flung away through diplomatic ineptitude. His life was
one magnificent parade, which, when ended, left only an
empty plain.

The King's heart was set upon the new Crusade. This
task seemed made for him. It appealed to every need of
his nature. To rescue the Holy Land from the pollution
of the infidel, to charge as a king at the head of knightly
squadrons in a cause at once glorious to man and espe-

cially acceptable to God, was a completely satisfying inspiration. The English would greatly have liked their King
to look after their affairs, to give them peace and order,
to nourish their growing prosperity, and to do justice
throughout the land. But they understood that the Crusade
was a high and sacred enterprise, and the Church taught
them that in unseen ways it would bring a blessing upon
them. Richard was crowned with peculiar state, by a ceremonial which, elaborating the most ancient forms and
tradition of the Island monarchy, is still in all essentials
observed to-day. Thereafter the King, for the sake of
Christ's sepulchre, virtually put the realm up for sale.
Money he must have at all costs for his campaign in far-
off Palestine. He sold and re-sold every office in the State.
He made new and revolutionarily heavy demands for taxa-
tion. He called for "scutage," or the commutation of military service for a money payment, and later re-introduced
"carucage," a levy on every hundred acres of land. Thus
he filled his chests for the Holy War.

A Justiciar was a King's deputy.

Confiding the government to two Justiciars, under the
supervision of the one trustworthy member of his family,
his mother, the old Queen, Eleanor of Aquitaine, he started
for the wars in the summer of 1190. After Richard had
marched across France and sailed to Sicily, where he rested
for the winter, his mother brought out to him Berengaria,
daughter of the King of Navarre, whom he had known
and admired, and now resolved to marry. It was fitting
that the "Lion-heart" should marry for love and not for
policy.

Navarre was a small independent kingdom in the Pyrenees between France and Spain.

The Anglo-French armies did not quit Sicily till the
spring of 1191. Richard paused in Cyprus. He quarrelled
with the local Greek ruler, declared that an insult had
been offered to his betrothed, conquered the island, and
there wedded Berengaria.

The glamours of chivalry illumine the tale of the Third
Crusade. All the chief princes of Europe were now in line
around the doomed stronghold of Saladin, rivalling each
other in prowess and jealousy. The sanctity of their cause
was no bar to their quarrels and intrigues. King Richard
dominated the scene. Fighting always in the most danger-

ous places, striking down the strongest foes, he negotiated all the time with Saladin. An agreement was in fact almost reached. To save his garrison Saladin offered to surrender his Christian captives, to pay a large indemnity, and to give up the cross, captured by him in Jerusalem, on which Christ—though this after twelve hundred years was not certain—had suffered. But the negotiations failed, and Richard in his fury massacred in cold blood the two thousand Turkish hostages who had been delivered as guarantees. Within five weeks of his arrival he brought the two years' siege to a successful conclusion.

By the time Acre fell King Richard's glory as a warrior and also his skill as a general were the talk of all nations. But the quarrels of the allies paralysed the campaign. Once again the distant prospect of Jerusalem alone rewarded the achievements of the Crusaders, and once again they fell back frustrated.

By now the news from England was so alarming that the King felt it imperative to return home. A peace or truce for three years was at length effected, by which the coastal towns were divided and the Holy Sepulchre opened as a place of pilgrimage to small parties of Crusaders. It was as tourists only that they reached their goal.

Richard's brother John was scheming to take his place.

Early in 1193 the King set out for home. Wrecked in the Adriatic, he sought to make his way through Germany in disguise, but his enemy the Duke of Austria was soon upon his track. He was arrested, and held prisoner in a castle. So valuable a prize was not suffered to remain in the Duke's hands. The Emperor himself demanded the famous captive. For many months his prison was a secret of the Imperial Court, but, as a pretty legend tells us, Blondel, Richard's faithful minstrel, went from castle to castle striking the chords which the King loved best, and at last was rewarded by an answer from Richard's own harp.

The Emperor of the Holy Roman Empire, of which Austria was a province.

Early in 1193, at a moment already full of peril, the grave news reached England that the King was prisoner "somewhere in Germany." There was general and well-founded consternation among the loyal bulk of his subjects. His brother John declared that Richard was dead, ap-

RICHARD I

The holy men of the European world, preaching to the medieval knights, send Richard with his caravans and ships off to the Third Crusade. Above is the siege of Acre; below, the massacre of the Turkish hostages. Richard dominates the Christian alliance and everywhere moves triumphantly, but in the end Jerusalem lies

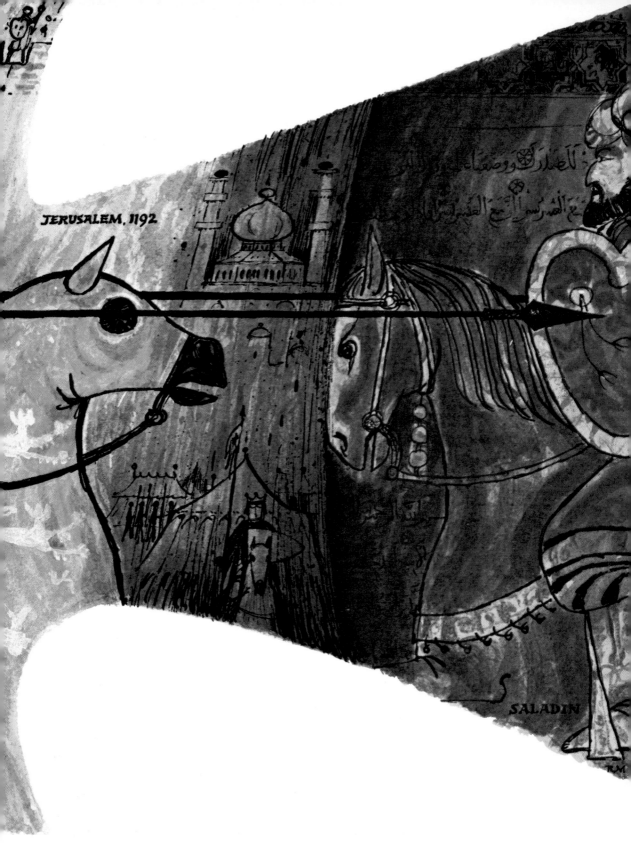

JERUSALEM, 1192

SALADIN

cold and forbidding in the distance as Saladin blocks the way to the Holy Land with his stubborn forces and with his faith in the Koran.

peared in arms, and claimed the crown. That England was held for Richard in his long absence against all these powerful and subtle forces is a proof of the loyalties of the feudal age. A deep sense of his heroic character and sacred mission commanded the allegiance of a large number of resolute, independent people whose names are unknown to history. The Church never flinched; the Queen-Mother with septuagenarian vigour stood by her eldest son; and the Council held the country. The coasts were guarded against an impending French invasion. John's forces melted. In April the strain was relieved by the arrival of authoritative news that Richard was alive. Prince John put the best face he could upon it and stole away to France.

If Queen Elizabeth II had to be ransomed today at a like rate, her price would be about twenty billion pounds or nearly fifty billion dollars.

The Holy Roman Emperor demanded the prodigious ransom of 150,000 marks, twice the annual revenue of the English Crown. One hundred thousand was to be ready in London before the King was liberated. Richard approved and the English Council agreed. Meanwhile King Philip of France and John were active on the other side. They offered the Emperor 150,000 marks to deliver the English King into their hands. But the Emperor felt that his blackmailing honour was engaged to Richard. Once Philip knew that the Emperor would not go back upon his bargain he sent John his notorious message: "Have a care—the Devil is unloosed."

It remained to collect the ransom. The charge staggered the kingdom. Yet nothing was more sacred than the feudal obligation to ransom the liege lord, above all when he enjoyed the sanctity of a Crusader. Three separate attempts were made to gather the money, and although England and Normandy, taxed to the limit, could not scrape together the whole of the 150,000 marks required, the Emperor, satisfied that he could get no more, resolved to set his captive at liberty.

At the end of 1193 the stipulated first instalment was paid, and at the beginning of February 1194 Richard Coeur de Lion was released from bondage. He picked his way, we may be assured, with care across Europe, avoiding his French domains, and in March arrived again in London among citizens impoverished but still rejoiced to see him and proud of his fame. He found John again in open rebellion, and Richard lent the weight of his strong right arm as well as the majesty of his name to the repression of the revolt. John fled once more to France. The King was recrowned in London with even more elaborate ceremony than before. These processes well started, he crossed the Channel to defend his French possessions. He never set foot in England again. But the Islanders owed him no grudge. All had been done as was right and due.

The mere arrival of the mighty warrior in France was enough to restore the frontiers and to throw King Philip and his forces upon an almost abject defensive. John sought pardon from the brother and liege lord he had so foully wronged. He did not sue in vain. With the full knowledge that if John had had his way he would still be a captive in a German castle, dethroned, or best of all dead—with all the long story of perfidy and unnatural malice in his mind, Coeur de Lion pardoned John, embraced him in fraternal love, and restored him to some of his estates, except certain fortresses which the barest prudence obliged him to reserve. This gesture was admired for its grandeur, though not perhaps for its wisdom, by the whole society, lay and spiritual, of Christendom.

*   *   *

The five remaining years of Richard's reign were spent in defending his French domains and raising money for that purpose from England.

Although Richard was an absentee King whose causes and virtues had proved a drain and disappointment to his subjects, his realm had not suffered so much as it would have seemed. It was proved that the King, to whom all allegiance had been rendered, was no longer the sole guarantee for law and order. There were other sureties upon which in addition the English nation could rely.

In France the King set himself during 1196 to build the most perfect fortress which his experience could devise. He called it Château Gaillard, or "Saucy Castle," and "my fair child;" and as it rose with all its outworks, bridges, and water-defenses into the immense triple-walled

stone structure which still scowls upon the roofs of Andelys
he rejoiced that it was beyond question the strongest fortress in the world. "If its walls were iron," said Philip in
his wrath, "I would take it." "If they were of butter," re-
torted Richard, "I would hold it." But fate was to give
Philip the last word.

In 1199, when the difficulties of raising revenue for the
endless war were at their height, good news was brought
to King Richard. It was said there had been dug up on
the lands of one of his vassals, a treasure of wonderful
quality; a group of golden images of an emperor, his wife,
sons, and daughters, seated round a table, also of gold,
had been unearthed. The King claimed this treasure as
lord paramount. The vassal lord resisted the demand, and
the King laid siege to his small, weak, castle. On the third
day, as he rode daringly near the wall, confident in his
hard-tried luck, a bolt from a crossbow near the wall
struck him in the left shoulder by the neck. The wound,
already deep, was aggravated by the necessary cutting out
of the arrow-head. Gangrene set in, and Coeur de Lion
knew that he must pay a soldier's debt. He prepared for
death with fortitude and calm, and in accordance with
the principles he had followed. He arranged his affairs; he
divided his personal belongings among his friends or be-
queathed them to charity. He sent for his mother, the redoubtable Eleanor, who was at hand. He declared John
to be his heir, and made all present swear fealty to him.
He ordered the archer who had shot the fatal bolt, and

In medieval romance Roland was the most celebrated fighting champion in Charlemagne's army. He had a wonderful horn called Olivant and a sword named Durandal which he had won from the giant Jutmundus. The horn could be heard at a distance of twenty miles. His exploits are set forth in the famous poem "Chanson de Roland," written about A.D. 1000.

who was now a prisoner, to be brought before him. He
pardoned him, and made him a gift of money. He received the offices of the Church with sincere and exemplary piety, and died in the forty-second year of his age
on April 6, 1199, worthy, by the consent of all men, to
sit with King Arthur and Roland and other heroes of martial romance at some Eternal Round Table, which we
trust the Creator of the Universe in His comprehension
will not have forgotten to provide.

The archer was flayed alive.

HENRY V

1387-1422

Henry V, the second of the Kings of the House of Lancaster, ascended the throne in 1413.

A GLEAM of splendour falls across the dark, troubled story of medieval England. Henry V was King at twenty-six. He felt, as his father had never done, sure of his title. He had spent his youth in camp and Council; he had for five or six years intermittently conducted the government of the kingdom during his father's decline. The romantic stories of his riotous youth and sudden conversion to gravity and virtue when charged with the supreme responsibility must not be pressed too far. It may well be true that "he was in his youth a diligent follower of idle practices, much given to instruments of music, and fired with the torches of Venus herself." But if he had thus yielded to the vehement ebullitions of his nature this was no more than a pastime, for always since boyhood he had been held in the grasp of grave business.

In the surging realm, with its ailing King, bitter factions, and deep social and moral unrest, all men had for some time looked to him; and succeeding generations have seldom doubted that according to the standards of his day he was all that a king should be. His face, we are told, was oval, with a long, straight nose, ruddy complexion, dark smooth hair, and bright eyes, mild as a dove's when unprovoked, but lion-like in wrath; his frame was slender, yet well-knit, strong and active. His disposition was orthodox, chivalrous and just. He came to the throne at a moment when England was wearied of feuds and brawl and yearned for unity and fame. He led the nation away from internal discord to foreign conquest; and he had the dream, and perhaps the prospect, of leading all Western Europe into the high championship of a Crusade. Council and Parliament alike showed themselves suddenly bent on war with France. As was even then usual in England, they wrapped this up in phrases of opposite import. Bishop Beaufort opened the session of 1414 with a sermon upon "Strive for the truth unto death" and the exhortation "While we have time, let us do good to all men." This was understood to mean the speedy invasion of France.

The Commons were thereupon liberal with supply. The King on his part declared that no law should be passed without their assent. A wave of reconciliation swept the

The phrase "opposite import" means that you are saying the reverse of what you mean.

John of Gaunt, father of King Henry IV, had a natural son Henry Beaufort, who became Bishop of Winchester in 1405 and was made a Cardinal by his half nephew Henry V in 1429. He presided over the court which sentenced Joan of Arc to the stake.

56

land. The King declared a general pardon. He sought to
assuage the past. He brought the body, or reputed body,
of Richard II to London, and reinterred it in Westminster
Abbey, with pageantry and solemn ceremonial. A plot
formed against him in the eve of his setting out for the
wars was suppressed, by all appearance with ease and national approval, and with only a handful of executions.
In particular he spared his cousin, the young Edmund
Mortimer, Earl of March, who had been named as the
rival King, through whose family much that was merciless
was to follow later.

During the whole of 1414 Henry V was absorbed in
warlike preparations by land and sea. He reorganised the
Fleet. Instead of mainly taking over and arming private
ships, as was the custom, he, like Alfred, built many vessels for the Royal Navy. He had at least six "great ships,"
with about fifteen hundred smaller consorts. The expedi-
tionary army was picked and trained with special care. In
spite of the more general resort to fighting on foot, which
had been compelled by the long-bow, six thousand archers,
of whom half were mounted infantry, were the bulk and
staple of the army, together with two thousand five hundred noble, knightly, or otherwise substantial warriors in
armour, each with his two or three attendants and aides.

In 1407 the Duke of Orleans, who was the decisive
power at the Court of the witless French King, Charles VI,
had been murdered at the instigation of the Duke of Burgundy, and the strife of the two parties which divided
France became violent and mortal. To this the late King
of England had owed the comparative relief from foreign
menace which eased the closing years of his reign. At
Henry V's accession the Orleanists had gained the pre-
ponderance in France, and unfurled the Oriflamme against
the Duke of Burgundy. Henry naturally allied himself with
the weaker party, the Burgundians, who, in their distress,
were prepared to acknowledge him as King of France.
When he led the power of England across the Channel
in continuation of the long revenge of history for Duke
William's expedition he could count upon the support of
a large part of what is now the French people. The Eng-

AGINCOURT.

RICHARD II

HARFLEUR

HENRY IV

KING HENRY THE FIFTH

After tragic times of peasant riots and the Black Death under Richard II and Henry IV, "a gleam of splendour falls across the dark, troubled story of medieval England." The crown now sits astride the Channel to dominate both France and England. Henry V sails across with his reorganized forces and the glory of his reign is con-

BATLE OF AGINCOURT 1415

summated in the epic battle of Agincourt where the English long-bowmen overwhelm the far more numerous forces of the French.

lish army of about ten thousand fighting men sailed to
France on August 11, 1415, in a fleet of small ships, and
landed without opposition at the mouth of the Seine. Harfleur was besieged and taken by the middle of September.
The King was foremost in prowess:

> Once more unto the breach, dear friends, once more;
> Or close the wall up with our English dead.

The term Dauphin designated the heir apparent to the throne of France, corresponding to the Prince of Wales in England. In this mood he now invited the Dauphin to end the war
by single combat. The challenge was declined. The attri-
tion of the siege, and disease, which levied its unceasing
toll on these medieval camps, had already wrought havoc
in the English expedition. The main power of France was
now in the field. The Council of War, on October 5, ad-
vised returning home by sea.

But the King, leaving a garrison in Harfleur, and sending home several thousand sick and wounded, resolved,
with about a thousand knights and men-at-arms and four
thousand archers, to traverse the French coast in a hun-
dred-mile march to his fortress at Calais, where his ships
were to await him. All the circumstances of this decision
show that his design was to tempt the enemy to battle.
This was not denied him. Falsely informed, he was deeply
plunged into France. The French army, which was already
interposing itself across his front, fell back before his advance-guard. Henry learned that they were before him in
apparently overwhelming numbers. He must now cut his
way through, perish, or surrender. When one of his officers
deplored the fact "that they had not but one ten thousand
of those men in England that do no work today," the
King rebuked him and revived his spirits in a speech to
which Shakespeare has given an immortal form:

> If we are marked to die, we are enough
> To do our country loss; and if to live,
> The fewer men, the greater share of honour.

"Wot you not," he actually said, "that the Lord with
these few can overthrow the pride of the French?" He and
the "few" lay for the night maintaining utter silence and
the strictest discipline. The French headquarters were at

Agincourt, and it is said that they kept high revel and diced for the captives they should take.

The English victory of Crécy was gained against great odds upon the defensive. Poitiers was a counter-stroke. Agincourt ranks as the most heroic of all the land battles England has ever fought. It was a vehement assault. The French, whose numbers have been estimated at about twenty thousand, were drawn up in three lines of battle, of which a proportion remained mounted. With justifiable confidence they awaited the attack of less than a third their number, who, far from home and many marches from the sea, must win or die. Mounted upon a small grey horse, with a richly jewelled crown upon his helmet, and wearing his royal surcoat of leopards and lilies, the King drew up his array. The archers were disposed in six wedge-shaped formations, each supported by a body of men-at-arms. At the last moment Henry gave the order, "In the name of Almighty God and of Saint George, Avaunt Banner in the best time of the year, and Saint George this day be thine help."

The French were unduly crowded upon the field. They stood in dense lines, and neither their cross-bowmen nor their battery of cannon could fire effectively. Under the arrow storm they in their turn moved forward down the slope, plodding heavily through a ploughed field already trampled into a quagmire. Still at thirty deep they felt sure of breaking the line. But once again the long-bow destroyed all before it. Horse and foot alike went down; a long heap of armoured dead and wounded lay upon the ground, over which the reinforcements struggled bravely, but in vain. In this grand moment the archers slung their bows, and, sword in hand, fell upon the reeling squadrons and disordered masses. Again they came and fell. Then perished the flower of the French nobility. The French third line quitted the field without attempting to renew the battle in any serious manner. Henry, who had declared at daybreak, "For me this day shall never England ransom pay," now saw his path to Calais clear before him. But far more than that: he had decisively broken in open battle at odds of more than three to one the armed chiv-

In 1346 at Crécy, 35,000 English under Edward III defeated 80,000 French under Philip VI.
In 1356 at Poitiers, 8,000 English under the Black Prince routed 60,000 French under King John.

alry of France. In two or at most three hours he had trodden underfoot at once the corpses of the slain and the willpower of the French monarchy.

After asking the name of the neighbouring castle and ordering that the battle should be called Agincourt after it, Henry made his way to Calais, short of food, but unmolested by the still superior forces which the French had set on foot. Within five months of leaving England he returned to London, having, before all Europe, shattered the French power by a feat of arms which, however it may be tested, must be held unsurpassed. He rode in triumph through the streets of London with spoils and captives displayed to the delighted people. He himself wore a plain dress, and he refused to allow his "bruised helmet and bended sword" to be shown to the admiring crowd, "lest they should forget that the glory was due to God alone." The victory of Agincourt made him the supreme figure in Europe.

This was the boldest bid the Island ever made in Europe. Henry V was no feudal sovereign of the old type with a class interest which overrode social and territorial barriers. He was entirely national in his outlook: he was the first King to use the English language in his letters and his messages home from the front; his triumphs were gained by English troops; his policy was sustained by a Parliament that could claim to speak for the English people. For it was the union of the country gentry and the rising middle class of the towns, working with the common lawyers, that gave the English Parliament thus early a character and a destiny that the States-General of France and the Cortes of Castile were not to know. Henry stood, and with him his country, at the summit of the world.

Ruthless he could be on occasion, but the Chroniclers prefer to speak of his generosity and of how he made it a rule of his life to treat all men with consideration. He disdained in State business evasive or cryptic answers. "It is impossible" or "It shall be done" were the characteristic decisions which he gave. He was more deeply loved by his subjects of all classes than any King has been in England. Under him the English armies gained an ascendancy which for centuries was never seen again.

When Henry revived the English claims to France he opened the greatest tragedy in our medieval history. Agincourt was a glittering victory, but the wasteful and useless campaigns that followed more than outweighed its military and moral value, and the miserable, destroying century that ensued casts its black shadow upon Henry's heroic triumph.

Fortune, which had bestowed upon the King all that could be dreamed of, could not afford to risk her handiwork in a long life. In the full tide of power and success he died at the end of August 1422 of a malady contracted in the field, probably dysentery, against which the medicine of those times could not make head. He died with his work unfinished. He had once more committed his country to the murderous dynastic war with France. He had been the instrument of the religious and social persecution of the Lollards. Perhaps if he had lived the normal span his power might have become the servant of his virtues and produced the harmonies and tolerances which mankind so often seeks in vain. But Death drew his scythe across these prospects. The gleaming King, cut off untimely, went to his tomb amid the lamentations of his people, and the crown passed to his son, an infant nine months old.

The followers of the celebrated religious leader John Wyclif were called Lollards.
Opposing the worship of images and other High-Church practices, they were the forerunners of Protestantism and of Puritanism.

JOAN OF ARC

1412-1431

A BABY WAS King of England, and two months later, on the death of Charles VI, was proclaimed without dispute the King of France. At the time of the great King's death the ascendancy of the English arms in France was established. The war continued bitterly. Nothing could stand against the English archers. Many sieges and much ravaging distressed the countryside.

Henry VI became King in 1422 at the age of nine months. His father's ruthless warriors still held most of France in subjugation.

The English attempt to conquer all vast France with a few thousand archers led by warrior nobles, with hardly any money from home, and little food to be found in the ruined regions, reached its climax in the triumph of Verneuil. There seemed to the French to be no discoverable way to contend against these rugged, lusty, violent Islanders, with their archery, their flexible tactics, and their audacity, born of victories great and small under varying conditions and at almost any odds. The defects of the Dauphin, the exhaustion of the French monarchy, and the disorder and misery of the realm had reached a pitch where all hung in the balance.

There now appeared upon the ravaged scene an Angel of Deliverance, the noblest patriot of France, the most splendid of her heroes, the most beloved of her saints, the most inspiring of all her memories, the peasant Maid, the ever-shining, ever-glorious Joan of Arc. In the poor, remote hamlet of Domremy, on the fringe of the Vosges Forest, she served at the inn. She rode the horses of travellers, bareback, to water. She wandered on Sundays into the woods, where there were shrines, and a legend that some day from these oaks would arise one to save France. In the fields where she tended her sheep the saints of God, who grieved for France, rose before her in visions. St. Michael himself appointed her, by right divine, to command the armies of liberation. Joan shrank at first from the awful duty, but when he returned attended by St. Margaret and St. Catherine, patronesses of the village church, she obeyed their command. There welled in the heart of the Maid a pity for the realm of France, sublime, perhaps miraculous, certainly invincible.

Like Mahomet, she found the most stubborn obstacle in her own family. Her father was scandalised that she

Mahomet (Mohammed) was opposed by his family when he proclaimed his revelations. In spite of this, they became the foundation of the Moslem religion.

should wish to ride in male attire among rough soldiers. How indeed could she procure horses and armour? How could she gain access to the King? But the saints no doubt felt bound to set her fair upon her course. She convinced Baudricourt, governor of the neighbouring town, that she was inspired. He recommended her to a Court ready to clutch at straws. She made a perilous journey across France. She was conducted to the King's presence in the immense stone pile of Chinon. There, among the nobles and courtiers in the great hall, under the flaring torches, she at once picked out the King, who had purposely mingled with the crowd. "Most noble Lord Dauphin," she said, "I am Joan the Maid, sent on the part of God to aid you and the kingdom, and by His order I announce that you will be crowned in the city of Rheims." Charles when the Maid picked him out among the crowd was profoundly moved. Alone with him, she spoke of State secrets which she must either have learned from the saints or from other high authority. She asked for an ancient sword which she had never seen, but which she described minutely before it was found. She fascinated the royal circle. When they set her astride on horseback in martial guise it was seen that she could ride. As she couched her lance the spectators were swept with delight.

For Charles of France, Churchill here uses the terms Dauphin and King interchangeably.

Policy now, if not earlier, came to play a part. The supernatural character of the Maid's mission was spread abroad. To make sure that she was sent by Heaven and not from elsewhere, she was examined by a committee of theologians, by the Parlement of Poitiers, and by the whole Royal Council. She was declared a virgin of good intent, inspired by God. Indeed, her answers were of such a quality that the theory has been put forward that she had for some time been carefully nurtured and trained for her mission. This at least would be a reasonable explanation of the known facts.

Orleans in 1429 lay under the extremities of siege. A few thousand English, abandoned by the Burgundians, were slowly reducing the city by an incomplete blockade. Their self-confidence and prestige hardened them to pursue the attack of a fortress deep in hostile territory, whose

The people of Burgundy, though French, were allies of the English.

garrison was four times their number. They had built lines of redoubts, within which they felt themselves secure. The Maid now claimed to lead a convoy to the rescue. In armour plain and without ornament, she rode at the head of the troops. She restored their spirits; she broke the spell of English dominance. She captivated not only the rough soldiery but their hard-bitten leaders. Her plan was simple. She would march straight into Orleans between the strongest forts. But the experienced captain, Dunois, a bastard of the late Duke of Orleans, had not proposed to lead his convoy by this dangerous route. As the Maid did not know the map he embarked his supplies in boats, and brought her by other ways into the besieged town almost alone. She was received with rapture. But the convoy, beaten back by adverse winds, was forced after all to come in by the way she had prescribed; and in fact it marched for a whole day between the redoubts of the English while they gaped at it dumbfounded.

The report of a supernatural visitant sent by God to save France, which inspired the French, clouded the minds and froze the energies of the English. The sense of awe, and even of fear, robbed them of their assurance. Dunois returned to Paris, leaving the Maid in Orleans. Upon her invocation the spirit of victory changed sides, and the French began an offensive which never rested till the English invaders were driven out of France. She called for an immediate onslaught upon the besiegers, and herself led the storming parties against them. Wounded by an arrow, she plucked it out and returned to the charge. She mounted the scaling-ladders and was hurled half stunned into the ditch. Prostrate on the ground, she commanded new efforts. "Forward, fellow-countrymen!" she cried. "God has delivered them into our hands." One by one the English forts fell and their garrisons were slain. The Earl of Suffolk was captured, the siege broken, and Orleans saved. The English retired in good order, and the Maid prudently restrained the citizens from pursuing them into the open country.

The Earl of Suffolk, William de la Pole, was later a leading politician under Henry VI and was executed in 1450.

Joan now was head indeed of the French army; it was dangerous even to dispute her decisions. The contingents from Orleans would obey none but her. She fought in fresh encounters; she led the assault upon Jargeau, thus opening the Loire above Orleans. In June 1429 she marched with the army that gained the victory of Patay. She told Charles he must march on Rheims to be crowned upon the throne of his ancestors. The idea seemed fantastic: Rheims lay deep in enemy country. But under her spell he obeyed, and everywhere the towns opened their gates before them and the people crowded to his aid. With all the pomp of victory and faith, with the most sacred ceremonies of ancient days, Charles was crowned at Rheims. By his side stood the Maid, resplendent, with her banner proclaiming the Will of God. If this was not a miracle it ought to be.

Joan now became conscious that her mission was exhausted; her "voices" were silent; she asked to be allowed to go home to her sheep and the horses of the inn. But all adjured her to remain. The French captains who conducted the actual operations, though restive under her military interference, were deeply conscious of her value to the cause. The Court was timid and engaged in negotiations with the Duke of Burgundy. A half-hearted attack was made upon Paris. Joan advanced to the fore-front and strove to compel victory. She was severely wounded and the leaders ordered the retreat. When she recovered she again sought release. They gave her the rank and revenue of an earl.

But the attitude both of the Court and the Church was changing towards Joan. Up to this point she had championed the Orleanist cause. After her "twenty victories" the full character of her mission appeared. It became clear that she served God rather than the Church, and France rather than the Orleans party. Indeed, the whole conception of France seems to have sprung and radiated from her. Thus the powerful particularist interests which had hitherto supported her were estranged. Meanwhile she planned to regain Paris for France. When in May 1430 the town of Compiegne revolted against the decision of the King that it should yield to the English, Joan with only six hundred men attempted its succour. She had no doubt that the enterprise was desperate. It took the form of a cavalry sortie across the long causeway over the river. The enemy, at first surprised, rallied, and a panic among the French ensued. Joan, undaunted, was bridled from the field by her friends. She still fought with the rearguard across the causeway. The two sides were intermingled. The fortress itself was imperilled. Its cannon could not fire upon the confused *mêlée*. Flavy, the governor whose duty it was to save the town, felt obliged to pull up the drawbridge in her face and leave her to the Burgundians.

She was sold to the rejoicing English for a moderate sum. To Bedford and his army she was a witch, a sorceress, a harlot, a foul imp of black magic, at all costs to

John of Lancaster, the Duke of Bedford, in command of the English armies in France, was the third son of Henry IV.

CHINON. 1429. JOAN AND THE DAUPHIN

Joan first hears the "voices" of the saints in the woods near her home at Domremy in central France.
Following their instructions, she goes to meet Charles the Dauphin in the great castle at Chinon where she
tells him she will free France and crown him King in Rheims. She marches forth in triumph, defeating the

JOAN OF ARC

BISHOP CAUCHON

ROUEN, 1431

English, but once victory is won she is betrayed and delivered into the hands of the enemy who imprison her, then bring her to trial as a witch. Finally she is burned at the stake as she holds a cross of twigs in her dying hands.

be destroyed. But it was not easy to frame a charge; she was a prisoner of war, and many conventions among the warring aristocrats protected her. The spiritual arm was therefore invoked. The Bishop of Beauvais, the learned doctors of Paris, pursued her for heresy. She underwent prolonged inquisition. The gravamen was that by refusing to disown her "voices" she was defying the judgment and authority of the Church. For a whole year her fate hung in the balance, while careless, ungrateful Charles lifted not a finger to save her. There is no record of any ransom being offered. Joan had recanted under endless pressure, and had been accorded all the mercy of perpetual imprisonment on bread and water. But in her cell the inexorable saints appeared to her again. Entrapping priests set her armour and man's clothes before her; with renewed exaltation she put them on. From that moment she was declared a relapsed heretic and condemned to the fire. Amid an immense concourse she was dragged to the stake in the market-place of Rouen. High upon the pyramid of faggots the flames rose towards her, and the smoke of doom wreathed and curled. She raised a cross made of firewood, and her last word was "Jesus!" History has recorded the comment of an English soldier who witnessed the scene. "We are lost," he said. "We have burnt a saint." All this proved true.

Joan was a being so uplifted from the ordinary run of mankind that she finds no equal in a thousand years. The records of her trial present us with facts alive to-day through all the mists of time. Out of her own mouth can she be judged in each generation. She embodied the natural goodness and valour of the human race in unexampled perfection. Unconquerable courage, infinite compassion, the virtue of the simple, the wisdom of the just, shone forth in her. She glorifies as she freed the soil from which she sprang. All soldiers should read her story and ponder on the words and deeds of the true warrior, who in one single year, though untaught in technical arts, reveals in every situation the key of victory.

HENRY VIII

1491-1547

Prince Arthur had died seven years before Henry became King in 1509.

Until the death of his elder brother, Prince Arthur, Henry had been intended for the Church. He had therefore been brought up by his father in an atmosphere of learning. Much time was devoted to serious studies— Latin, French, Italian, theology, music—and also to bodily exercise, to the sport of jousting, at which he excelled, to tennis, and hunting the stag. His manner was straightforward and owing to his father's careful savings he had at his accession more ready money than any other prince in Christendom.

Henry in his maturity was a tall, red-headed man who preserved the vigour and energy of ancestors accustomed for centuries to the warfare of the Welsh marches. His massive frame towered above the throng, and those about him felt in it a sense of concealed desperation, of latent force and passion. A French ambassador confessed, after residing for months at Court, that he could never approach the King without fear of personal violence. Although Henry appeared to strangers open, jovial, and trustworthy, with a bluff good humour which appealed at once to the crowd, even those who knew him most intimately seldom penetrated the inward secrecy and reserve which allowed him to confide freely in no one. To those who saw him often he seemed almost like two men, one the merry monarch of the hunt and banquet and procession, the friend of children, the patron of every kind of sport, the other the cold, acute observer of the audience chamber or the Council, watching vigilantly, weighing arguments, refusing except under the stress of great events to speak his own mind. On his long hunting expeditions, when the courier arrived with papers, he swiftly left his companions of the chase and summoned the "counsellors attendant" for what he was wont to call "London business."

Bursts of restless energy and ferocity were combined with extraordinary patience and diligence. Deeply religious, Henry regularly listened to sermons lasting between one and two hours, and wrote more than one theological treatise of a high standard. He was accustomed to hear five Masses on Church days, and three on other days, served the priest at Mass himself, was never deprived of holy bread and holy water on Sunday, and always did penance on Good Friday. His zeal in theological controversy earned him from the Pope the title of "Defender of the Faith." An indefatigable worker, he digested a mass of dispatches, memoranda, and plans each day without the help of his secretary. He wrote verses and composed music. Profoundly secretive in public business, he chose as his advisers men for the most part of the meanest origin: Thomas Wolsey, the son of a poor and rascally butcher of Ipswich, whose name appears on the borough records for selling meat unfit for human consumption; Thomas Cromwell, a small attorney; Thomas Cranmer, an obscure lecturer in divinity. Like his father he distrusted the hereditary nobility, preferring the discreet counsel of men without a wide circle of friends.

Early in his reign he declared, "I will not allow anyone to have it in his power to govern me." As time passed his wilfulness hardened and his temper worsened. His rages were terrible to behold. There was no noble head in the country, he once said, "but he would make it fly," if his will were crossed. Many heads were indeed to fly in his thirty-eight years on the throne.

This enormous man was the nightmare of his advisers. Once a scheme was fixed in his mind he could seldom be turned from it; resistance only made him more stubborn. His habit was to talk to all classes—barbers, huntsmen, his "yeoman cook to the King's mouth"—and particularly anyone, however humble, connected with the sea, to ferret out opinions, and ride off on hunting expeditions which sometimes lasted for weeks. He showed himself everywhere. Each summer he went on progress through the country, keeping close to the mass of his subjects, whom he understood so well.

Almost the first act, six weeks after the death of his father in 1509, was to marry his brother Arthur's widow, Princess Catherine of Aragon. He was aged eighteen and she was five years and five months older. She had made great efforts to fascinate him, and succeeded so well that there can be no doubt that Henry was eager to complete the proceedings. Catherine was at Henry's side during the first twenty-two years of his reign, while England was becoming a force in European affairs, perilous for foreign rulers to ignore. Until she reached the age of thirty-eight she remained, apart from three or four short lapses, the mistress of his affections, restrained his follies, and in her narrow way helped to guide public affairs between the intervals of her numerous confinements. Henry settled down to married life very quickly, in spite of a series of misfortunes which would have daunted a less robust character. The Queen's first baby was born dead, just after Henry's nineteenth birthday; another died soon after birth a year later. In all there were to be five such disappointments.

*   *   *

The King continued the standing alliance with his father-in-law, Ferdinand of Aragon, which had brought honour and wealth to England. He supported the Pope, and was sent the Golden Rose, the highest distinction which could be conferred on any Christian prince. He deliberated with his father's grave counsellors—and under their guidance pursued for a short time the policy which his father always favoured—isolation, provided that France continued to pay tribute. But Henry was on the edge of the vortex of Europe's new politics. Should he plunge in? The richest cities of Europe had changed hands many times during the last few years, paying tribute on each occasion. Frontiers were altering almost from month to month. Amid the alluring vistas of conquest which opened up before Henry his father's aged counsellors remained obstinately men of peace. Henry VII had only once sent English levies abroad, preferring to hire mercenaries who fought alongside foreign armies. Henry VIII now determined that this policy should be reversed.

The Hundred Years War between France and England came to a close after the burning of Joan in 1430. So a truce of nearly another hundred years had occurred before this time.

The year was 1512, and this was the first time since the Hundred Years War that an English army had campaigned in Europe. But the expedition to Gascony failed. The English found that the style of warfare they had learned in the Wars of the Roses, with long-bows and ponderously armed mounted men, had become obsolete on the Continent. After negotiations lasting throughout the winter of 1512–13 Ferdinand and the Venetians deserted Henry and the Pope and made peace with France. The Holy League, they concluded, although high-sounding in name, had proved futile as a political combination. But Henry VIII and the Pope never wavered. Pope Julius II, who had been besieged by a French force in Rome, had excommunicated the entire French army, and now grew a beard, an adornment then out of fashion, and swore he would not shave until he was revenged on the King of France. Henry, not to be outdone, also grew a beard. It was auburn, like his hair. Their arrangements, though costly, were brilliantly successful. Under Henry's command, the English with Austrian mercenaries, routed the French in August 1513 at the Battle of the Spurs, so called because of the rapidity of the French retreat. To crown all, Queen Catherine, who had been left behind as Regent of England, sent great news from the North. At Flodden Field on the Scottish border, a bloody battle was fought on September 9, 1513. The whole of Scotland, Highland and Lowland alike, drew out with their retainers in the traditional schiltrons, or circles of spearmen, and around the standard of their King. The English archers once again directed upon these redoubtable masses a long, intense, and murderous arrow storm. When night fell the flower of the Scottish chivalry lay in their ranks where they had fought, and among them King James IV.

Fitting celebrations were arranged in Brussels. Henry, now twenty-two, was permitted to spend whole nights dancing "in his shirt" with the leading beauties of the Imperial Court. "In this," the Milanese Ambassador reported, "he performs wonders, leaping like a stag." The Council had forbidden gaming and the presence of women in the English lines, but "for him," the Ambassador added, "the Austrians provide everything." His rewards were princely; he never sat down to the table without losing in a royal manner, and the chief personalities were gratified with rich presents.

The King's popularity rose with the achievements of his reign. There were many of course who grumbled at

Thomas Wolsey was made Lord Chancellor and Cardinal in 1515 and soon afterward became Prime Minister of Henry VIII.

the war taxes imposed during the previous two years; but while pouring money into pageantry and magnificence Wolsey managed to tap new sources of revenue. Henry's subjects were taxed much as they had been under his father, which was more lightly than any other subjects in Europe.

Within a few years of his accession Henry embarked upon a programme of naval expansion, while Wolsey concerned himself with diplomatic manoeuvre. Henry had already constructed the largest warship of the age, the *Great Harry,* of 1,500 tons, with "seven tiers one above the other, and an incredible array of guns." The fleet was built up under the personal care of the sovereign, who ordered the admiral to send word to him in minute detail "how every ship did sail," and was not content until England commanded the Narrow Seas.

The Narrow Seas was a popular term for the English Channel.

The zenith of this brilliant period was reached at the Field of the Cloth of Gold in June 1520, when Henry crossed the Channel to meet his rival, Francis I of France, for the first time. Henry's main perplexity was, we are told, about his appearance; he could not decide how he would look best, in his beard as usual or clean-shaven. At first he yielded to Catherine's persuasion and shaved. But directly he had done so he regretted the step and grew the beard again. It reached its full luxuriance in time to create a great impression in France.

At the Field of the Cloth of Gold, near Guisnes, the jousting and feasting, the colour and glitter, the tents and

trappings, dazzled all Europe. It was the last display of medieval chivalry. Many noblemen, it was said, carried on their shoulders their mills, their forests, and their meadows. But Henry and Francis failed to become personal friends. Henry, indeed, was already negotiating with Francis's enemy, the new Emperor Charles V, who had lately succeeded his grandfather, Maximilian. At Guisnes he attempted to outdo Francis both by the splendour of his equipment and the cunning of his diplomacy. Relying on his great physical strength, he suddenly challenged Francis to a wrestling match. Francis seized him in a lightning grip and put him on the ground. Although the ceremonies continued Henry could not forgive such a personal humiliation.

*   *   *

In 1525 Queen Catherine was aged forty. At the Field of the Cloth of Gold, five years before, King Francis had mocked at her behind the scenes with his courtiers. A typical Spanish princess, she had matured and aged rapidly; it was clear that she would bear Henry no male heir. Would England accept Catherine's child, Mary, now aged nine, as the first Queen of England in her own right since Matilda? It was doubtful if a woman could succeed to the throne by English law.

We first hear of Anne Boleyn at Court in a dispatch dated August 16, 1527, four months after Henry had begun proceedings for the annulment of his marriage. Did he plan the divorce and then find Anne? Or had he arranged to marry Anne from the beginning? We shall never know, for Henry was very secretive in his private matters. "Three may keep counsel," he observed a year or two later, "if two be away; and if I thought my cap knew my counsel I would cast it into the fire and burn it."

*   *   *

The winter of 1531–32 was marked by the tensest crisis of Henry's reign. A form of excommunication, or even interdict, had been drafted in Rome, ordering the King to cast off his concubine Anne within fifteen days, only the penalties being left blank. The shadow of Papal wrath hung over England. But, as in the dark days in the early part of the reign, the King pursued his inflexible course to the end. Opposition merely confirmed him in his plans.

Having established his supremacy, Henry proceeded to exploit it. In March 1533 the Duke of Norfolk with royal commissioners waited on Queen Catherine. Every sort of reason was advanced why she should renounce her title voluntarily. She refused to resign. Then she was informed of the decisions of Convocation. Steps would be taken to deprive her of the rank of Queen, to which she was no longer entitled. She declared her determination to resist. But the Commissioners had still another announcement to make. Catherine was in any case Queen no longer, for the King was already married to Anne Boleyn.

Thomas Cranmer, largely through Henry's influence, was appointed Archbishop of Canterbury in 1533 and he annulled Catherine's marriage shortly afterward.

Thus Henry's secret marriage became known. A fortnight later Cranmer opened a court at Dunstable, citing Catherine to appear. She refused. In her absence the Archbishop pronounced judgment. Catherine's marriage with Henry had existed in fact but not in law; it was void from the beginning; and five days afterwards the marriage with Anne was declared valid. Queen Anne Boleyn was crowned on June 1 in Westminster Abbey.

The following month it became clear that the new Queen was expecting a child. A magnificent and valuable bed, which had lain in the Treasury since it had formed part of a French nobleman's ransom, was brought forth, and in it on September 7, 1533, the future Queen Elizabeth was born.

Although bonfires were lighted there was no rejoicing in Henry's heart. A male heir had been his desire. After he had defied the whole world, perhaps committed bigamy, and risked deposition by the Pope and invasion, here was only a second daughter. He galloped at once away from Greenwich, away from Anne, and in three days had reached the residence of a worthy old courtier, Sir John Seymour, who had a clever son in the diplomatic service and a pretty daughter, a former Maid of Honour to Queen Catherine. Jane Seymour was about twenty-five, and although she was attractive no one considered her a great beauty. But she was gay, and generally liked, and Henry fell in love with her.

After the birth of Elizabeth criticism of the King and his ecclesiastical measures could no longer be stifled. If the choice was between two princesses, men said, then why not choose Mary, the legitimate one? But the King would have none of this argument. An Act was passed vesting the succession in Elizabeth. In March 1534 every person of legal age, male or female, throughout the kingdom was forced to swear allegiance to this Act and renounce allegiance to all foreign authority in England. To publish or pronounce maliciously by express words that the King was a tyrant or heretic was made high treason. As the brutality of the reign increased many hundreds were to be hanged, disembowelled, and quartered on these grounds.

Fisher and Sir Thomas More, who both refused the oath, were confined in the Tower for many months. At his trial More offered a brilliant defence, but the King's former trust in him had now turned into vengeful dislike. Under royal pressure the judges pronounced him guilty of treason. While Fisher was in the Tower the Pope created seven cardinals, of whom one was "John, Bishop of Rochester, kept in prison by the King of England." Directly Henry heard the news he declared in anger several times that he would send Fisher's head to Rome for the Cardinal's hat. Fisher was executed in June 1535 and More in July. For their fate the King must bear the chief responsibility; it is a black stain on his record. Shortly afterwards Henry was excommunicated and in theory deprived of his throne by the Pope.

John Fisher, Bishop of Rochester, was one of the most prominent supporters of the new learning and a friend of the famous Dutch scholar Erasmus, but he was hostile to the Reformation.

Thomas More was an eminent English statesman and author of Utopia. *He was beatified, that is declared a saint, by Pope Leo XIII in 1886.*

The resistance of More and Fisher to the royal supremacy in Church government was a noble and heroic stand. They realised the defects of the existing Catholic system, but they hated and feared the aggressive nationalism which was destroying the unity of Christendom. They saw that the break with Rome carried with it the threat of a despotism freed from every fetter. More stood forth as the defender of all that was finest in the medieval outlook. He represents to history its universality, its belief in spiritual values, and its instinctive sense of other-worldliness.

Henry boldly displays on his massive chest many portraits of the personages of his incredible reign. His father holds the red rose of Lancaster; his mother the white rose of York; Henry himself the golden rose from Rome. His brother and two sisters are here, and of course his six wives and three children; also his three powerful ministers and Sir Thomas More, who became his rival. Above are scenes of his youth as

TOWER OF LONDON

"GREAT HARRY"

THE "GREAT BIBLE"

THOMAS CROMWELL

ANNE OF CLEVES

EDWARD VI

MARY I   ELIZABETH I

THOMAS CRANMER

CATHERINE HOWARD

CATHERINE PARR

hunter, scholar, jouster, musician. The Great Harry *symbolizes the navy. The Tower of London is a symbol of his cruel executions, and the "Great Bible" one of his glorious gifts to his people. The white space signifies his break with the Roman Church.*

Henry VIII with cruel axe decapitated not only a wise and gifted counsellor, but a system which, though it had failed to live up to its ideals in practice, had for long furnished mankind with its brightest dreams.

*   *   *

The King was still paying court to Jane Seymour when it became known that Anne was expecting another baby. But this time Henry refused to have anything to do with her. She was haggard and ill and had lost her freshness. The King instead of pitying her, gave way to an uncontrollable outburst of rage. Jane Seymour was installed at Greenwich.

In January 1536 Queen Catherine died. If the King was minded to marry again he could now repudiate Queen Anne without raising awkward questions about his earlier union. It was already rumoured by the Seymour party that in her intense desire for an heir Queen Anne had been unfaithful to the King soon after the birth of Elizabeth, with several lovers. If proved, this offence was capital. The following Sunday a certain Smeaton, a gentleman of the King's chamber, who played with great skill on the lute, was arrested as the Queen's lover. Smeaton subsequently under torture confessed to the charge. At the conclusion of the proceedings the Queen was placed under arrest, and kept under guard until the tide turned to take her up-river to the Tower. She was charged with being unfaithful to the King; and other offences, including incest with her brother. The Queen denied the charges vigorously, and replied to each one in detail. The peers retired, and soon returned with a verdict of guilty: the Queen was to be burnt or beheaded, at the King's pleasure.

Anne received the sentence with calm and courage. She declared that if the King would allow it she would like to be beheaded like the French nobility, with a sword, and not, like the English nobility, with an axe. Her wish was granted. "Pray for me," she said, and knelt down while one of the ladies-in-waiting bandaged her eyes. Before there was time to say a Paternoster she bowed her head, murmuring in a low voice, "God have pity on my

The Lord's Prayer is so called because in Latin "pater noster" are its first two words, meaning "our father."

soul." "God have mercy on my soul," she repeated, as the executioner stepped forward and slowly took his aim. Then the great blade hissed through the air, and with a single stroke his work was done.

As soon as the execution was known Henry appeared in yellow, with a feather in his cap, and ten days later was privately married to Jane Seymour at York Place. Jane proved to be the submissive wife for whom Henry had always longed. Anne had been too dominating and too impulsive. Jane was the opposite, gentle though proud; and Henry spent a happy eighteen months with her. She was the only Queen whom Henry regretted and mourned, and when she died, still aged only twenty-two, immediately after the birth of her first child, the future Edward VI, Henry had her buried with royal honours in St. George's Chapel at Windsor. He himself lies near her.

Though all had been bliss at Court while Jane was Queen rural England was heavy with discontents. Henry was increasingly short of revenue and Church properties offered a tempting prize. The religious orders had for some time been in decline, and parents were becoming more and more averse to handing over their sons to the cloisters. At some houses the monks had given up all hope of carrying on, and squandered the endowments, cutting down woods, pawning the plate, and letting the buildings fall into disrepair or ruin. Grave irregularities had been discovered. Parliament made little difficulty about winding up the smaller houses, when satisfied that their inmates were either to be transferred to large houses or pensioned off. During the summer of 1536 royal commissioners toured the country, completing the dissolution as swiftly as possible.

The King had now a new chief adviser. As First Minister Cromwell handled the dissolution of the monasteries with conspicuous, cold-blooded efficiency. It was a step which appealed to the well-to-do. The high nobility and country gentry acquired on favourable terms all kinds of fine estates. The King was thus assured of the support of the Parliament and the prosperous classes. Most of the displaced monks, nearly ten thousand in all, faced their lot with re-

Thomas Cromwell, Earl of Essex, the son of a blacksmith who became Lord High Chamberlain of England in 1539, was beheaded on the charge of treason in 1540.

lief or fortitude, assisted by substantial pensions. Some even married nuns, and many became respectable parish clergy. The dissolution brought lands into the Crown's possession worth at the time over £100,000 a year, and by the sale or lease of the rest of the former monastic properties the Crown gained a million and a half—a huge sum for those days, though probably much less than the properties were worth. The main result of this transaction was in effect, if not in intention, to commit the landed and mercantile classes to the Reformation settlement and the Tudor dynasty.

In 1534 the Act of Supremacy appointing the King and his successors Protector and only Supreme Head of the Church and Clergy of England is considered the beginning of the English Reformation, the decisive break with Rome, and the severance of the Anglican and Roman Catholic Churches.

In the field of religious belief the Reformation brought profound change. The Bible now acquired a new and far-reaching authority. The Government commissioned in Paris a great printing of English Bibles, more sumptuous than any previous edition, and in September 1538 directed that every parish in the Country should purchase a Bible of the largest volume in English, to be set up in each church, where the parishioners might most commodiously resort to the same and read it. Six copies were set up in St. Paul's, in the City of London, and multitudes thronged the cathedral all day to read them, especially, we are told, when they could get any person that had an audible voice to read aloud. This Bible has remained the basis of all later editions, including the Authorised Version prepared in the reign of James I.

The King was now a widower. One Continental house he considered marrying into was the Duchy of Cleves, which to some extent shared his own attitude in religion, hating the Papacy, yet restricting Lutheranism. An alliance with the princes of Northern Germany against the two Catholic monarchs now seemed imperative, and negotiations for a marriage between Henry and Anne, the eldest Princess of Cleves, were hurried on. Anne's charms, Cromwell reported, were on everybody's lips. Anne spoke only German, spent her time chiefly in needlework, and could not sing or play any instrument. She was thirty years old, very tall and thin, with an assured and resolute countenance, slightly pockmarked, but was said to possess wit and animation, and did not over-indulge in beer.

Anne spent Christmas at Calais, waiting for storms to abate, and on the last day of the year 1539 arrived at Rochester. Henry had sailed down in his private barge, in disguise, bearing a fine sable fur among the presents. On New Year's Day he hurried to visit her. But on seeing her he was astonished and abashed. At last he said very sadly and pensively, "I see nothing in this woman as men report of her, and I marvel that wise men should have made such report as they have done." Privately he dubbed her "the Flanders Mare."

But the threat from abroad compelled the King to fulfil his contract. Since he now knew as much about the Canon Law on marriage as anyone in Europe, he turned himself into the perfect legal example of a man whose marriage might be annulled. The marriage was never consummated. Henry was merely waiting, watching the European situation, until it was safe to act.

In June 1540 yet another of Norfolk's nieces, Catherine Howard, was presented to Henry and captured his affections at first sight. Anne agreed to have her marriage annulled, and Convocation pronounced it invalid. She lived on in England, pensioned and in retirement, for another seventeen years. A few days after Cromwell was executed on July 28 Henry was privately married to his fifth wife, Catherine Howard.

Convocation was the parliament of the clergy.

Catherine, about twenty-two, with auburn hair and hazel eyes, was the prettiest of Henry's wives. His Majesty's spirits revived, his health returned, and he went down to Windsor to reduce weight.

But wild, tempestuous Catherine was not long content with a husband nearly thirty years older than herself. Her reckless love for her cousin, Thomas Culpeper, was discovered, and she was executed in the Tower in February 1542 on the same spot as Anne Boleyn. The night before the execution she asked for the block so that she could practise laying her head upon it, and as she mounted the scaffold said, "I die a Queen, but would rather die the wife of Culpeper. God have mercy on my soul."

Henry's sixth wife, Catherine Parr, was a serious little widow from the Lake District, thirty-one years of age,

ENGLAND
Windsor Greenwich
Berkshire London
Surrey Calais
Portsmouth
the Solent Isle of Wight
English Channel
FRANCE

learned and interested in theological questions, who had
had two husbands before the King. She married Henry
at Hampton Court on July 12, 1543, and until his death
three years later made him an admirable wife, nursing his
ulcerated leg, which grew steadily worse and in the end
killed him. She contrived to reconcile Henry with the future
Queen Elizabeth; both Mary and Elizabeth grew fond of
her, and she had the fortune to outlive her husband.

*　　*　　*

The brilliant young Renaissance prince had grown old
and wrathful. The pain from his leg made Henry ill-tem-
pered; he suffered fools and those who crossed him with
equal lack of patience. Suspicion dominated his mind and
ruthlessness marked his actions. At the time of his marriage with Catherine Parr he was engaged in preparing
the last of his wars. The roots of the conflict lay in Scotland.

Henry's position was extremely grave. Without a single
ally, the nation faced the possibility of invasion from both
France and Scotland. The crisis called for unexampled
sacrifices from the English people; never had they been
called upon to pay so many loans, subsidies, and benev-
olences. To set an example Henry melted down his own
plate and mortgaged his estates. At Portsmouth he prepared for the threatened invasion in person. A French
fleet penetrated the Solent and landed troops in the Isle
of Wight; but they were soon driven off, and the crisis
gradually passed. The war in the North smouldered on,
yielding no definite results. Henry completely failed in
Scotland. He would make no generous settlement with his
neighbours, yet he lacked the force to coerce them.

In 1546 Henry was as yet only fifty-five. In the autumn
he made his usual progress through Surrey and Berkshire
to Windsor, and early in November he came up to London. He was never to leave his capital alive again.

Henry's rule saw many advances in the growth and
the character of the English state, but it is a hideous blot
upon his record that the reign should be widely remembered for its executions. Two Queens, two of the King's

chief Ministers, a saintly bishop, numerous abbots, monks and many ordinary folk who dared to resist the royal will were put to death. Almost every member of the nobility in whom royal blood ran perished on the scaffold at Henry's command. Roman Catholic and Calvinist alike were burnt for heresy and religious treason. These persecutions, inflicted in solemn manner by officers of the law, perhaps in the presence of the Council or even the King himself, form a brutal sequel to the bright promise of the Renaissance. The sufferings of devout men and women among the faggots, the use of torture, and the savage penalties imposed for even paltry crimes, stand in repellent contrast to the enlightened principles of humanism. Yet his subjects did not turn from Henry in loathing. He succeeded in maintaining order amid the turmoil of Europe without army or police, and he imposed on England a discipline which was not attained elsewhere. A century of religious wars went by without Englishmen taking up arms to fight their fellow-countrymen for their faith. We must credit Henry's reign with laying the basis of sea-power, with a revival of Parliamentary institutions, with giving the English Bible to the people, and above all with strengthening a popular monarchy under which succeeding generations worked together for the greatness of England while France and Germany were racked with internal strife.

GOOD QUEEN BESS

1533-1603

MARY, QUEEN OF SCOTS

THE EARL OF LEICESTER

KING PHILIP OF SPAIN

JOHN HAWKINS

SIR FRANCIS DRAKE

THE SPANISH ARMADA

THE EARL OF ESSEX

SIR WALTER RALEIGH

ELIZABETH WAS twenty-five years old when, untried in the affairs of State, she succeeded her half-sister, Mary, on November 17, 1558. It was England's good fortune that the new Queen was endowed by inheritance and upbringing with a combination of very remarkable qualities. There could be no doubt who her father was. A commanding carriage, auburn hair, eloquence of speech, and natural dignity proclaimed her King Henry's daughter. Other similarities were soon observed: high courage in moments of crisis, a fiery and imperious resolution when defied, and an almost inexhaustible fund of physical energy. She enjoyed many of the same pastimes and accomplishments as the King had done—a passion for the chase, skill in archery and hawking, and in dancing and music. She could speak six languages, and was well read in Latin and Greek. As with her father and grandfather, a restless vitality led her hither and thither from mansion to mansion, so that often none could tell where in a week's time she might be sleeping.

A difficult childhood and a perilous adolescence had been Elizabeth's portion. At one stage in her father's lifetime she had been declared illegitimate and banished from Court. During Mary's reign, when her life might have been forfeited by a false step, she had proved the value of caution and dissemblance. When to keep silence, how to bide her time and husband her resources, were the lessons she learnt from her youth. Many historians have accused her of vacillation and parsimony. Certainly these elements in her character were justly the despair of her advisers. The royal treasury however was never rich enough to finance all the adventurous projects urged upon her. Nor was it always unwise amid the turbulent currents of the age to put off making irrevocable decisions. The times demanded a politic, calculating, devious spirit at the head of the state, and this Elizabeth possessed. She had, too, a high gift for picking able men to do the country's work. It came naturally to her to take the credit for their successes, while blaming them for all that went wrong.

In quickness of mind the Queen was surpassed by few of her contemporaries, and many envoys to her Court had

Henry VIII had been dead for eleven years. His only son, Edward VI, succeeded him but died after only six years and Mary, daughter of Henry's first Queen, Catherine of Aragon, reigned for the next five years.

91

good reason to acknowledge her liveliness of repartee. In temperament she was subject to fits of melancholy, which alternated with flamboyant merriment and convulsive rage. Always subtle of intellect, she was often brazen and even coarse in manners and expression. When angered she could box her Treasurer's ears and throw her slipper in her Secretary's face. She was outwardly very free in her more tender relations with the opposite sex, so that, in the words of an illustrious counsellor, "one day she was greater than man, and the next less than woman." Nevertheless she had a capacity for inspiring devotion that is perhaps unparalleled among British sovereigns. There may be something grotesque to modern eyes in the flattery paid her by the Court, but with her people she never went wrong. By instinct she knew how to earn popular acclaim. In a sense her relationship with her subjects was one long flirtation. She gave to her country the love that she never entirely reposed in any one man, and her people responded with a loyalty that almost amounted to worship. It is not for nothing that she has come down to history as Good Queen Bess.

Few sovereigns ever succeeded to a more hazardous inheritance than she. England's link with Spain had brought the loss of Calais and the hostility of France. Tudor policy in Scotland had broken down. The old military danger of the Middle Ages, a Franco-Scottish alliance, again threatened. In the eyes of Catholic Europe, Mary, the Queen of Scots, and wife of the Dauphin of France, who became King Francis II in 1559, had a better claim to the English throne than Elizabeth, and with the power of France behind her she stood a good chance of gaining it. Even before the death of Henry VIII, England's finances had been growing desperate. English credit at Antwerp, the centre of the European money market, was so weak that the Government had to pay 14 per cent for its loans. The coinage, which had been debased yet further under Edward VI, was now chaotic. England's only official ally, Spain suspected the new regime for religious reasons.

Elizabeth had been brought up a Protestant. She was a paragon of the New Learning. Around her had gathered some of the ablest Protestant minds. Religious peace at home and safety from Scotland were the foremost needs of the realm. England became Protestant by law, Queen Mary's Catholic legislation was repealed, and the sovereign was declared supreme Governor of the English Church. But this was not the end of Elizabeth's difficulties. New ideas were in debate, not only on religious doctrine and Church government, but on the very nature and foundations of political power.

It is at this point that the party known as the Puritans, who were to play so great a role in the next hundred years, first enter English history. Democratic in theory and organisation, intolerant in practice of all who differed from their views, the Puritans challenged the Queen's authority in Church and State, and although she sought for freedom of conscience and could maintain with sincerity that she "made no windows into men's souls," she dared not let them organise cells in the body religious or the body politic. A discordant and vigorous minority could rupture the delicate harmony that she was patiently weaving. Protestantism must be saved from its friends.

One thing seemed certain to all contemporaries. The security of the English State depended in the last resort on an assured succession. The delicate question of the Queen's marriage began to throw its shadow across the political scene, and it is in her attitude to this challenge that the strength and subtleties of Elizabeth's character are revealed. The country was well aware of the responsibility which lay upon her. If she married an Englishman her authority might be weakened, and there would be fighting among the suitors. The perils of such a course were borne in on her as she watched the reactions of her Court to her long and deep affection for the handsome, ambitious Robert Dudley whom she made Earl of Leicester. This was no way out. During the first months of her reign she had also to consider the claims of her brother-in-law, Philip II of Spain. A Spanish marriage had brought disaster to her sister, but marriage to Philip might buy a powerful friend; refusal might drive his religious animosity into the open. But by 1560 she had achieved a temporary

security and could wait her time. Marriage into one of
the reigning houses of Europe would mean entangling herself in its European policy and facing the hostility of her
husband's rivals. In vain the Houses of Parliament begged
their Virgin Queen to marry and produce an heir. Elizabeth was angry. She would admit no discussion. Her policy
was to spend her life in saving her people from such a
commitment, and using her potential value as a match to
divide a European Combination against her.

*   *   *

Meanwhile there was Mary Stuart, Queen of Scots.
Her young husband, King Francis II, of France, had died
shortly after his accession, and in December 1560 she returned to her own kingdom.

Mary Stuart was a very different personality from
Elizabeth, though in some ways her position was similar.
She was a descendant of Henry VII; she held a throne;
she lived in an age when it was a novelty for a woman
to be the head of a state; and she was now unmarried.
But the Queen of Scots lacked the vigilant self-control
which Elizabeth had learnt in the bitter years of childhood. Mary's marriage points the contrast between the
two sovereigns. Elizabeth had seen and avoided the danger
of choosing a husband from her Court. Mary had only
been a few years in Scotland when she married her cousin,
Henry Stuart, Lord Darnley, a weak, conceited youth who
had both Tudor and Stuart blood in his veins. The result
was disaster. The old feudal factions, now sharpened by
religious conflict, seized Scotland in their grip. Mary's
power melted slowly and steadily away. Her husband became a tool of her opponents. In desperation she connived
at his murder, and in 1567 married his murderer, a warlike Border lord, Bothwell, whose unruly sword might yet
save her throne and her happiness. But defeat and imprisonment followed, and in 1568 she escaped into England and threw herself upon the mercy of the waiting
Elizabeth.

Mary in England proved even more dangerous than
Mary in Scotland. She became the focus of plots and con-

spiracies against Elizabeth's life. The survival of Protestant England was menaced by her existence. For nearly twenty years the uneasy struggle continued with Spanish plots, revolt in the Low Countries and especially the sudden massacre of the Huguenots on the eve of the feast of St. Bartholomew, August 23, 1572, enhancing the general turmoil.

This general massacre of French Protestants who were called Huguenots was touched off by the marriage of Henry of Bourbon, King of Navarre, with the sister of Charles IX, Margaret of Valois. Henry saved himself by pretending to be converted to Catholicism.

At length the conspiracies focused upon the person of Mary Queen of Scots, long captive. She was the heir to the English throne in the event of Elizabeth's removal from the world. Elizabeth herself was reluctant to recognise the danger to her life, yet the plots sharpened the question of who should succeed to the English throne. The death of Mary would make her son James the heir to the crown of England, and James was in safe Calvinist hands in Scotland. To avoid having another Catholic Queen it was only necessary to dispose of Mary before the Jesuits, or their allies, disposed of Elizabeth. In 1585 evidence of a conspiracy was laid before the Council. An agent had mingled with the conspirators for over a year. Mary's connivance was undeniable. Elizabeth was at last persuaded that her death was a political necessity. After a formal trial Mary was pronounced guilty of treason. Parliament petitioned for her execution, and Elizabeth at last signed the death warrant.

The Jesuits were the most militant branch of the Catholics.

The scene of Mary's death has caught the imagination of history. In the early morning of February 8, 1587, she was summoned to the great hall of Fotheringay Castle. Accompanied by six of her attendants, she awaited the servants of the English Queen. From the neighbouring countryside the gentry gathered to witness the sentence. Mary appeared at the appointed hour soberly clad in black satin. In the quietness of the hall she walked with stately movements to the cloth-covered scaffold erected by the fireplace. The solemn formalities were smoothly completed. But the zealous Dean of Peterborough attempted to force upon the Queen a last-minute conversion. With splendid dignity she brushed aside his loud exhortations. "Mr Dean," she said, "I am a Catholic, and must die a Catholic. It is useless to attempt to move me, and your prayers will avail me but little."

The cathedral at Peterborough was one of the oldest and finest in England.

Mary had arrayed herself superbly for the final scene. As she disrobed for the headsman's act, her garments of black satin, removed by the weeping handmaids, revealed a bodice and petticoat of crimson velvet. One of her ladies handed her a pair of crimson sleeves, which she put on. Thus the unhappy Queen halted, for one last moment, standing blood-red from head to foot against the black background of the scaffold. There was a deathly hush throughout the hall. She knelt, and at the second stroke the final blow was delivered. The awed assembly had fulfilled its task. In death the majestic illusion was shattered. The head of an ageing woman with false hair was held up by the executioner. A lapdog crept out from beneath the clothes of the bleeding trunk.

As the news reached London bonfires were lit in the streets. Elizabeth sat alone in her room, weeping more for the fate of a Queen than a woman. The responsibility for this deed she shifted with an effort on to the shoulders of her masculine advisers.

War was now certain. The chances were heavily weighted in favour of Spain. From the mines of Mexico and Peru there came a stream of silver and gold which so fortified the material power of the Spanish Empire that King Philip could equip his forces beyond all known scales. The position was well understood in the ruling circles of England. So long as Spain controlled the wealth of the New World she could launch and equip a multitude of Armadas; the treasure must therefore be arrested at its source or captured from the ships which conveyed it across the oceans. In the hope of strengthening her own finances and harassing the enemy's preparations against the Netherlands and ultimately against herself, Elizabeth had accordingly sanctioned a number of unofficial expeditions against the Spanish coasts and colonies in South America. These had continued for some time, and as yet without open declaration of war, but she had come to realise that scattered raids of which she professed no prior knowledge could do no lasting harm to the Spanish Empire beyond the seas or the Spanish power in Northern Europe. Gradually therefore these expeditions had assumed an official

character, and the Royal Navy surviving from the days of
Henry VIII was rebuilt and reorganised by John Hawkins,
son of a Plymouth merchant, who had formerly traded
with the Portuguese possessions in Brazil. Hawkins had
learnt his seamanship in slave-running on the West African
coast and in shipping Negroes to the Spanish colonies. In
1573 he was appointed Treasurer and Controller of the
Navy. He had moreover educated an apt pupil, a young
adventurer from Devon, Francis Drake.

This "Master Thief of the unknown world," as his
Spanish contemporaries called Drake, became the terror
of their ports and crews. His avowed object was to force
England into open conflict with Spain, and his attacks on
the Spanish treasure ships, his plundering of Spanish possessions on the western coast of the South American continent on his voyage round the world in 1577, and raids
on Spanish harbours in Europe, all played their part in
driving Spain to war. From their experiences on the Spanish Main the English seamen knew they could meet the
challenge so long as reasonable equality was maintained.
With the ships that Hawkins had built they could fight
and sink anything the Spaniards might send against them.

The Spaniards had long contemplated an enterprise
against England. They realised that English intervention
threatened their attempts to reconquer the Netherlands
and that unless England was overwhelmed the turmoil
might continue indefinitely. Preparations were delayed by
Drake's famous raid on Cadiz in 1587. In this "singeing
of the King of Spain's beard" a large quantity of stores
and ships was destroyed. Nevertheless in May 1588 the
Armada was ready. A hundred and thirty ships were assembled, carrying 2,500 guns and more than 30,000 men,
two-thirds of them soldiers.

Hawkins's work for the Navy was now to be tested.
News of their approach off the Lizard was brought into
Plymouth harbour on the evening of July 19. The English
fleet had to put out of the Sound the same night against
light adverse winds which freshened the following day. If
the Spanish Admiral, Medina-Sidonia, had attacked the
English vessels to leeward of his ships as they struggled to

In delicate majesty, Elizabeth points with one hand to the worldly achievements of her explorers, while the other hand gives her hesitant decision of death for Mary Queen of Scots. The four men mostly responsible for the flaming defeat of the Spanish Armada are contrasted to the popular saying which credited the natural

LORD HOWARD

R MARTIN FROBISHER

SIR JOHN HAWKINS

SIR FRANCIS DRAKE

1588 + GOD BLEW AND THEY WERE SCATTERED

PHILIP II

EARL OF ESSEX

SIR WALTER RALEIGH

VIRGINIA

forces that dashed so many of the ships to pieces in gales off the Irish Coast. Above is Philip of Spain, who died soon after learning of his defeat. Two of the ambitious younger men of Elizabeth's court, Essex and Raleigh, stand forth gallantly toward the end of her reign, but both were later to be beheaded.

clear the land on the Saturday there would have been a disaster for the English. But his instructions bound him to

sail up the Channel, unite with the Duke of Parma, and help transport to England the veteran troops already assembled near Dunkirk.

A further engagement followed on the 25th off the Isle of Wight. It looked as if the Spaniards planned to seize the island as a base. But as the westerly breeze blew stronger the English still lay to windward and drove them once more to sea in the direction of Calais, where Medina, ignorant of Parma's movements, hoped to collect news. Medina then made a fatal mistake. He anchored in Calais Roads. The Queen's ships which had been stationed in the eastern end of the Channel joined the main fleet in the straits, and the whole sea-power of England was now combined. A council of war held in the English flagship during the evening of July 28 resolved to attack. The decisive engagement opened. After darkness had fallen eight ships from the eastern squadron which had been filled with explosives and prepared as fire-ships—the torpedoes of those days—were sent against the crowded Spanish fleet at anchor in the roads. Lying on their decks, the Spanish crews must have seen unusual lights creeping along the decks of strange vessels moving towards them. Suddenly a series of explosions shook the air, and flaming hulks drifted towards the anchored Armada. The Spanish captains cut their cables and made for the open sea. Collisions without num-

ber followed. One of the largest galleys, the *San Lorenzo,* lost its rudder and drifted aground in Calais harbour, where the Governor interned the crew. The rest of the fleet with a south-south-west wind behind it, made eastwards.

The tormented Armada now sailed northwards out of the fight. Their one aim was to make for home. The horrors of the long voyage round the north of Scotland began. Not once did they turn upon the small, silent ships which followed them in their course. Neither side had enough ammunition.

The homeward voyage of the Armada proved the qualities of the Spanish seamen. Facing mountainous seas and racing tides, they escaped from their pursuers. Their ships had been shattered by the English cannonades and now were struck by the autumn gales. Seventeen went ashore. Nevertheless over sixty-five ships, about half of the fleet that had put to sea, reached Spanish ports during the month of October. The English had not lost a single ship, and scarcely a hundred men. But their captains were disappointed. There were no boastings; they recorded their dissatisfactions.

But to the English people as a whole the defeat of the Armada came as a miracle. For thirty years the shadow of Spanish power had darkened the political scene. A wave of religious emotion filled men's minds. One of the medals struck to commemorate the victory bears the inscription *"Afflavit Deus et dissipantur"*—"God blew and they were scattered."

Elizabeth and her seamen knew how true this was. The Armada had indeed been bruised in battle, but it was demoralised and set on the run by the weather. Yet the event was decisive. The English seamen might well have triumphed. Though limited in supplies and ships the new tactics of Hawkins had brought success. The nation was transported with relief and pride.

With 1588 the crisis of the reign was past. England had emerged from the Armada year as a first-class Power. She had resisted the weight of the mightiest empire that had been seen since Roman times. Her people awoke to a consciousness of their greatness, and the last years of Elizabeth's

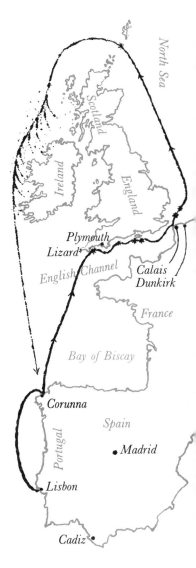

THE ARMADA ROUTE

reign saw a welling up of national energy and enthusiasm focusing upon the person of the Queen. Poets and courtiers alike paid their homage to the sovereign who symbolised the great achievement. Elizabeth had schooled a generation of Englishmen.

The success of the seamen pointed the way to wide opportunities of winning wealth and fame in daring expeditions. The young men who now rose to prominence in the Court of the ageing Queen plagued their mistress to allow them to try their hand in many enterprises. The coming years resound with attacks upon the forces and allies of Spain throughout the world—expeditions to Cadiz, to the Azores, into the Caribbean Sea, to the Low Countries, and in support of the Huguenots, to the northern coasts of France. The policy of the English Government was to distract the enemy in every quarter of the world, and by subsidising the Protestant elements in the Low Countries and in France to prevent any concentration of force against themselves.

But as the conflict with Spain drew inconclusively on, and both sides struck at each other in ever-growing, offensive exhaustion, the heroic age of sea fights passed away.

Victory over Spain was the most shining achievement of Elizabeth's reign, but by no means the only one. The repulse of the Armada had subdued religious dissension at home. Events which had swung England towards Puritanism while the Catholic danger was impending swung her back to the Anglican settlement when the peril vanished in the smoke of the burning Armada. And bitter as the coming divisions were to be, England united in prizing Elizabeth's service to her people and to religion.

By now, the men who had governed England since the 1550's were passing from power and success to their graves. The fifteen years which followed the Armada are dominated by other figures. War with Spain had set a premium on martial virtues. Young and eager men like Walter Raleigh and Robert Devereux, Earl of Essex, quarreled for permission to lead enterprises against the Spaniards. The Queen hesitated. She knew that the security she had striven for all her life was very fragile. She knew the danger of provoking the might of Spain, backed as it was by all the wealth of the Indies. She was growing old and out of touch with the younger generation, and her quarrel with Essex marked and revealed her changing mood.

The Queen's favour had lighted upon the hard, handsome, and ambitious Captain of the Guard, Sir Walter Raleigh. But Essex was the younger and the more fiery, and he soon displaced the Captain in the affections of Elizabeth. He too was ambitious, and set out to create his own party in Court and Council. In 1593 he was made a Privy Counsellor. In 1596 an expedition was sent against Cadiz under the joint command of Essex and Raleigh. In the sea fight for the harbour Raleigh was the outstanding leader. The Spanish fleet was burned and the town lay open to the English crews. Essex was the hero of the shore fight. It was a brilliant combined operation, and Cadiz was held by the English for a fortnight. The fleet returned home triumphant, but, to Elizabeth's regret, little the richer.

Victory at Cadiz heightened the popularity of Essex among the younger members of the Court and throughout the country. He was given command of an expedition to intercept a further Armada now gathering in the ports of Western Spain. Raleigh too was in the expedition. But the English failed to take any of the island ports; the Spanish Treasure Fleet eluded them; the Armada put out into the Bay of Biscay with the seas clear of defending ships to the north. Once again the winds saved the Island. The badly manned galleons tottered into a northern gale scattered and sinking. The disorganised fleet crept back into its ports. King Philip was kneeling in his chapel in the Escorial praying for his ships. Before the news of their return could reach him he was seized with a paralytic stroke, and the tale of their failure was brought to him on his deathbed.

The Escorial is a famous building near Madrid containing a palace, monastery, museum, church, and royal mausoleum.

Essex came home to find a sovereign still vigorous and dominating. The muddle and quarreling which had marred the Azores expedition enraged Elizabeth. She declared she would never send the Fleet out of the Channel again, and this time she kept her word. Essex retired from Court, and thunderous days followed. Angry scenes occurred between Essex and the Queen, and the Earl was confined to his house. Weeks dragged by, and a desperate plot was made by Essex and his younger companions.

The scheme failed, and the end came in February 1601 with Essex's death on Tower Hill. Among the witnesses of the execution was Walter Raleigh. Silently Raleigh walked across to the door of the White Tower and climbed the stairway through the armoury, to look down upon the block where he too, last of the Elizabethans, was to meet the same end.

Elizabeth well understood the issues at stake. Essex had been not simply a courtier soliciting, and even fighting for, the affections of his Queen. He was the leader of a bid for power by a faction of her Court. Long years of statesmanship served Elizabeth better than the driving ambition of a courtier half her age. She struck back; and in destroying Essex she saved England from the consumption of civil war.

If Essex challenged the political power of Elizabeth, more significant for the future was the challenge to her constitutional power in the Parliament of 1601. But the Queen forestalled the direct challenge, and in a golden speech to a large gathering of her Commons summoned to her chamber she told them, "Though God hath raised me high, yet this I account the glory of my crown, that I have reigned with your loves." It was to be her last appearance in their midst.

The immense vitality displayed by the Queen throughout the troublous years of her rule in England ebbed slowly and relentlessly away. She lay for days upon a heap of cushions in her room. For hours the soundless agony was prolonged. The corridors without echoed with the hurrying of agitated feet. At last Robert Cecil dared to speak. "Your Majesty, to content the people you must go to bed." "Little man," came the answer, "is 'must' a word to use to princes?" The old Archbishop of Canterbury, Whitgift, her "little black husband," as she had once called him, knelt praying at her side. In the early hours of the morning of March 24, 1603, Queen Elizabeth died.

GEORGE WASHINGTON

1732-1799

Canada

Maine •
(to Mass.)

New Hampshire •
New York •
Massachusetts •
Connecticut •
Pennsylvania •
New Jersey •
Rhode
Island
Maryland • Delaware

Virginia •

North Carolina •

• South Carolina

• Georgia

THE
AMERICAN
COLONIES
1775

Florida (Spanish)

Washington had led the troops of Virginia against French and Indian raids.

IN MAY 1775 a congress of delegates from the American colonies met in the Carpenters' Hall of the quiet Pennsylvanian town of Philadelphia. They were respectable lawyers, doctors, merchants, and landowners, nervous at the onrush of events, and seemingly unfitted to form a revolutionary committee. The first shots had been fired and blood had been shed, but all hope of compromise had not yet vanished, and they were fearful of raising a military Power which might overwhelm its creators. They had no common national tradition except that against which they were revolting, no organisation, no industries, no treasury, no supplies, no army. Many of them still hoped for peace with England. In Britain George III alone seemed to favour force. The great Pitt, former Prime Minister was saying to the House of Commons, "My Lords if I were an American as I am an Englishman, while a foreign troop was landed in my country I never would lay down my arms—never, never, never." Yet British troops under General Sir William Howe were on their way across the Atlantic, and armed, violent, fratricidal conflict stared them in the face.

It was imperative for the Patriots to raise an army. Massachusetts had already appealed to Congress at Philadelphia for help against the British and for the appointment of a Commander-in-Chief. Two days before the action at Bunker Hill Congress had agreed. There had been much talk of whom they were to choose. There was jealousy and dislike of the New Englanders, who were bearing the brunt of the fighting, and largely for political reasons it was decided to appoint a Southerner. Adams's eye centred upon a figure in uniform, among the dark brown clothes of the delegates. He was Colonel George Washington of Mount Vernon, Virginia. This prosperous planter had fought in the campaigns of the 1750's and had helped extricate the remnants of Braddock's force from their disastrous advance. He was the only man of any military experience at the Congress, and this was limited to a few minor campaigns on the frontier. He was now given command of all the forces that America could raise. Great calls were to be made on the spirit of resolution that was his by nature.

His immediate task was to provide the ragged band at
Boston with discipline and munitions, and to this he devoted the autumn and winter months of 1775. The war
was to be fought with great odds against him. At the end
of every campaign there were many desertions. Short of
clothing and shelter, they shivered and grumbled through
the winter months. Often the Patriot cause seemed lost.
But Washington remained alert and undaunted and fortune eventually rewarded him. Simply to have kept his
army in existence during these years was probably Washington's greatest contribution to the Patriot cause. No
other American leader could have done as much.

*   *   *

When the War of Independence was over the Thirteen
Colonies were free to make their own lives. The struggle
had told heavily upon their primitive political organisation. The Articles of Confederation to which they had
subscribed in 1777 set up a weak central Government en-
joying only such authority as the Americans might have
allowed to the British Crown. Their Congress had neither
the power nor the opportunity in so vast a land of creating an ordered society out of the wreckage of revolution
and war.

In March 1789 the new Federal bodies were convened.
Opponents of the Constitution exulted in the difficulties
of gathering a quorum in the Upper and Lower House.
There seemed little vigour and enthusiasm in the new
regime. But by the end of the month sufficient people had
arrived in New York, where the Government was to meet.
The first step was to elect a President, and General Washington, the commander of the Revolution, was the obvious
choice. Disinterested and courageous, far-sighted and patient, aloof yet direct in manner, inflexible once his mind
was made up, Washington possessed the gifts of character
for which the situation called. He was reluctant to accept
office. Nothing would have pleased him more than to remain in equable but active retirement at Mount Vernon,
improving the husbandry of his estate. But, as always, he
answered the summons of duty. Gouverneur Morris was

right when he emphatically wrote to him, "The exercise of authority depends on personal character. Your cool, steady temper is *indispensably necessary* to give firm and manly tone to the new Government."

There was much confusion and discussion on titles and precedence, which aroused the mocking laughter of critics. But the prestige of Washington lent dignity to the new, untried office. On April 30, 1789, in the recently opened Federal Hall in New York, he was solemnly inaugurated as the first President of the United States. A week later the French States-General met at Versailles. Another great revolution was about to burst upon a bewildered world. The flimsy, untested fabric of American unity and order had been erected only just in time.

As yet there were no administrative departments. These were quickly set up: Treasury, State, and War. The success of the new Federal Government depended largely upon men chosen to fill these key offices: Alexander Hamilton, the great Federalist from New York; Thomas Jefferson, the Virginia democrat, now returned from Paris; and, to a lesser extent, General Knox of Massachusetts.

From 1789 to his resignation six years later Hamilton used his brilliant abilities to nourish the Constitution and bind the economic interests of the great merchants of America to the new system. A governing class must be created, and Hamilton proposed to demonstrate that Federal government meant a strong national economy. The moneyed interest was overjoyed by his programme, but there was bitter opposition from those who realised that the new Government was using its taxing powers to pay interest to the speculative holders of state debts now assumed by Congress. The clash between capitalist and agrarian now glared forth.

This cleavage is of durable importance in American history. The beginnings of the great political parties can be discerned, and they soon found their first leaders. Hamilton was quickly recognised as head of the financial and mercantile interest centring in the North, and his opponent was none other than Jefferson, Secretary of State. The two men had worked together during the first months of the new Government. Hamilton indeed had only secured enough votes for the passage of his proposals on state debts by winning Jefferson's support. This he did by agreeing that the new capital city which would house Congress and Government should be sited on the Potomac River, across the border from Virginia. In the meantime Philadelphia was to succeed New York as the temporary capital. But a wave of speculation which followed the financial measures of Hamilton now aroused the Secretary's opposition. The two leaders misunderstood each other fundamentally. Washington, impressed by the need to stabilise the new Constitution, exerted his weighty influence to prevent an open rupture.

The outward unity of the Federal administration was preserved for a few months by the re-election of Washington as President. But the conflict between Jefferson and Hamilton was not confined to economics. A profoundly antagonistic view of politics separated them. They held radically opposed views of human nature. Hamilton, the superbly successful financier, believed that men were guided by their passions and their interests, and that their motives, unless rigidly controlled, were evil. "The people!" he is supposed to have said. "The people is a great beast." Majority rule and government by the counting of heads were abhorrent to him. There must be a strong central Government and a powerful governing circle, and he saw in Federal institutions, backed by a ruling class, the hope and future of America. The developing society of England was the ideal for the New World, and such he hoped to create across the Atlantic by his efforts at the Treasury Department. He represents and symbolises one aspect of American development, the successful, self-reliant business world, with its distrust of the collective common man, of what Hamilton himself in another mood called "the majesty of the multitude." But in this gospel of material success there was little trace of that political idealism which characterises and uplifts the American people. "A very great man," President Wilson was to call him, adding with evident bias, "but not a great American."

Thomas Jefferson was the product of wholly different

On a background of the British flag are shown King George III and the three ministers who were chiefly responsible for the stamp tax that ignited the American War of Independence. In the transitional sections are pictured well-known scenes of the war: the Boston Tea Party, Paul Revere's ride, and various other incidents

YORKTOWN   OCTOBER 17, 1781

FRENCH ALLIANCE

SERAPIS + BONHOMME RICHARD

SEPTEMBER 23, 1779

BURGOYNE
OCT 14, 1777

MOUNT VERNON

GEORGE WASHINGTON

leading to the victory that created the new American flag. This becomes a background for George Washington, father of his country, with a medallion of his house at Mount Vernon where he spent his most peaceful and his last days.

conditions and the prophet of a rival political idea. He came from the Virginian frontier, the home of dour individualism and faith in common humanity, the nucleus of resistance to the centralising hierarchy of British rule. Jefferson had been the principal author of the Declaration of Independence and leader of the agrarian democrats in the American Revolution. He was well read; he nourished many scientific interests, and he was a gifted amateur architect. His graceful classical house, Monticello, was built according to his own designs. He was in touch with fashionable Left-Wing circles of political philosophy in England and Europe, and, like the French school of economists who went by the name of Physiocrats, he believed in a yeoman-farmer society. He feared an industrial proletariat as much as he disliked the principle of aristocracy. Industrial and capitalist development appalled him. He despised and distrusted the whole machinery of banks, tariffs, credit manipulation, and all the agencies of capitalism which the New Yorker Hamilton was skilfully introducing into the United States. He perceived the dangers to individual liberty that might spring from the centralising powers of a Federal Government. With reluctance he came home from Paris to serve the new system. The passage of time and the stress of the Napoleonic wars were to modify his dislike of industrialism, but he believed in his heart that democratic government was only possible among free yeomen. It was not given to him to foresee that the United States would eventually become the greatest industrial democracy in the world.

Jefferson held to the Virginian conception of society, simple and unassailed by the complexity, the perils, and the challenge of industrialism. In France he saw, or thought he saw, the realisation of his political ideas—the destruction of a worn-out aristocracy and a revolutionary assertion of the rights of soil-tilling man. Hamilton, on the other hand, looked to the England of the Younger Pitt as the embodiment of his hopes for America. The outbreak of war between England and France was to bring to a head the fundamental rivalry and conflict between Hamilton and Jefferson and to signalise the birth of the great American parties, Federalist and Republican. Both were to split and founder and change their names, but from them the Republican and Democratic parties of to-day can trace their lineage.

The convulsion which shook France in 1789 was totally different from the revolutions that the world had seen before. England in the seventeenth century had witnessed a violent shift in power between the Crown and the People; but the basic institutions of State had been left untouched, or at any rate had soon been restored. Nor as yet had there been in England any broadening of popular sovereignty in the direction of universal suffrage. The liberties of the ordinary Englishman were well understood and had often been asserted. He could not lay claim to equality. The lack was not felt to be a very serious grievance, since the classes mingled together and transition from one class to another was, if not easy, at least possible, and quite often achieved. America in her Revolution had proclaimed the wider rights of mankind. Across the Atlantic shone a noble example of freedom which in the end was to exercise a formidable influence upon the world. But in the late eighteenth century America's commanding future was scarcely foreseen, even by her own statesmen. In Europe the impulse towards liberty, equality, and popular sovereignty had to come from elsewhere. It came from France. The English Revolution had been entirely a domestic affair. So in the main had the American. But the French Revolution was to spread out from Paris across the whole Continent. It gave rise to a generation of warfare, and its echoes reverberated long into the nineteenth century and afterwards. Every great popular and national movement, until the Bolsheviks gave a fresh turn to events in 1917, was to invoke the principles set forth at Versailles in 1789.

The confused and tumultuous issues of European politics reached America in black and white. Debate on the French Revolution raged throughout the country. Corresponding societies on the Revolutionary model sprang up wherever Jeffersonian principles were upheld, while the Federalist Press thundered against the Jacobins of the New World, and denounced them as destroyers of society.

The Bolsheviks were the extremists of the early revolutionary party in Russia. They finally gained power under Lenin, Trotsky, and Stalin.

A group of French revolutionists was called the Jacobins from the Jacobin (St. Jacques) convent in Paris where they met. Originally moderate, the society was speedily taken over by the violent leaders of the Revolution, of which Robespierre was the most notorious.

Controversy became less theoretical and much more vehement as soon as American commercial interests were affected. Tempers rose as American ships and merchandise endured the commerce-raiding and privateering of France and Britain. Both parties demanded war—the Federalists against France and the Jeffersonians against England. President Washington was determined to keep the infant republic at peace. His task was smoothed by the antics of the French Revolutionary envoy to the United States, Citizen Genêt, who, finding the Government reluctant to honour the Franco-American alliance of 1778, meddled in American politics, attempted to raise troops, and greatly embarrassed his political allies. In August 1793 Washington demanded his recall. But, knowing the sharp activity of the guillotine in France, Genêt wisely married an American heiress and subsided peaceably in the New World.

Washington prevailed, and it was he who enunciated the first principle of traditional American foreign policy. In April 1793 his famous proclamation of neutrality declared that it was "the disposition of the United States to pursue a conduct friendly and impartial towards the belligerent Powers." But relations with Britain were clouded by unsettled issues. Hamilton's Federalist Party was deeply committed to maintaining a friendly commerce with Britain. The farmers and pioneers of the frontier felt differently. To them, Britain was the enemy who refused to honour the treaty of 1783 by evacuating the frontier posts on the Canadian border, and was pushing her fur trade from Canada southwards, inciting the Indians against American settlers, and threatening the flank of their own advance to the West. The British in their turn resented the failure of the American Government to settle the large debts still unpaid since before the Revolution. Meanwhile British interference with American shipping, on the plea that it was helping to sustain France, stung public opinion throughout the United States.

Washington decided that the whole field of Anglo-American relations must be revised and settled, and in 1794 he appointed John Jay, Chief Justice of the Supreme Court, as Envoy Extraordinary to London. The British

Government felt little tenderness for their late rebels. They knew their military weakness, and Washington's need of the support of Hamilton's party. Moreover, they were considerably aided by Jay's ineptitude in negotiation. A treaty was drawn up which made few concessions to America. The treaty revealed and exposed the superiority of British diplomacy and the weakness of the new American Government. The atmosphere was charged afresh with distrust, and the seeds were sown for another war between Britain and the United States.

Washington's second term of office expired in the spring of 1797, and he prepared longingly for his retirement to Mount Vernon. His last days in power were vexed by the gathering assaults of the anti-Federalists and the din of preparations for the new Presidential election. Washington and many of his associates were alarmed by the growth of party spirit. They clung to the view that the diverse interests of the nation were best reflected in a balanced and all-embracing Government. The notion that two great parties should perpetually struggle for power was foreign and repellent to them. Only Jefferson, who had already resigned from the administration, had a clear vision of the role that parties should play. He saw the advantages of directing the strife of factions into broad streams and keeping an organised Opposition before the country as a possible alternative Government. But in Washington's mind the dangers of faction were uppermost when in September he issued his Farewell Address to the nation. This document is one of the most celebrated in American history. It is an eloquent plea for union, a warning against "the baneful effects of the Spirit of Party." It is also an exposition of the doctrine of isolation as the true future American policy. "Europe has a set of primary interests, which to us have none, or a very remote relation. Hence she must be engaged in frequent controversies, the causes of which are essentially foreign to our concerns. Hence therefore it must be unwise in us to implicate ourselves by artificial ties in the ordinary vicissitudes of her politics or the ordinary combinations and collisions of her friendships or enmities. Our detached and distant situation invites us to pursue a different course . . . 'Tis our true policy to steer clear of permanent alliances with any portion of the foreign world . . . Taking care always to keep ourselves, by suitable establishments, in a respectable defensive posture, we may safely trust to temporary alliances for extraordinary emergencies."

 George Washington holds one of the proudest titles that history can bestow. He was the Father of his Nation. Almost alone his staunchness in the War of Independence held the American colonies to their united purpose. His services after victory had been won were no less great. His firmness and example while first President restrained the violence of faction and postponed a national schism for sixty years. His character and influence steadied the dangerous leanings of Americans to take sides against Britain or France. He filled his office with dignity and inspired his administration with much of his own wisdom. To his terms as President are due the smooth organisation of the Federal Government, the establishment of national credit, and the foundation of a foreign policy. By refusing to stand for a third term he set a tradition in American politics which has only been departed from by President Roosevelt in the Second World War.

For two years Washington lived quietly at his country seat on the Potomac, riding round his plantations, as he had long wished to do. Amid the snows of the last days of the eighteenth century he took to his bed. On the evening of December 14, 1799, he turned to the physician at his side, murmuring, "Doctor, I die hard, but I am not afraid to go." Soon afterwards he passed away.

HORATIO NELSON

1758-1805

O<small>N THE CONTINENT</small> the French were everywhere triumphant. Bonaparte, dominant in Western Europe, firmly planted in the Mediterranean, safeguarded against attack from Germany by a secret understanding with Austria, had only to consider what he would conquer next. A sober judgment might have said England, by way of Ireland. Bonaparte thought he saw his destiny in a larger field. In the spring of 1798 he sailed for Egypt. Nelson sailed after him.

During the afternoon of August 1 a scouting vessel from Nelson's fleet signalled that a number of French battleships were anchored to the east of Alexandria close in to the shallow water, with dangerous shoals to port. The French Admiral was convinced that not even an English admiral would risk sailing his ship between the shoals and the French line. But Nelson knew his captains. As evening drew near, five British ships passed in succession on the land side of the enemy, while Nelson, in the *Vanguard*, led the rest of his fleet to lie on the starboard of the French line.

The French sailors were many of them on shore and the decks of their vessels were encumbered with gear. They had not thought it necessary to clear the gun ports on their landward side. In the rapidly falling darkness confusion seized their fleet. Relentlessly the English ships, distinguished by four lanterns hoisted in a horizontal pattern, battered the enemy van, passing from one disabled foe to the next down the line. Of the great fleet that had convoyed Napoleon's army to the adventure in Egypt only two ships of the line and two frigates escaped.

Nelson's victory of the Nile cut Napoleon's communications with France and ended his hopes of vast Eastern conquests. In 1799 he escaped back to France, leaving his army behind him. The British Fleet was once again supreme in the Mediterranean Sea. This was a turning-point.

Since the renewal of war Britain had found herself alone against Napoleon, and for two years she maintained the struggle single-handed during one of the most critical periods in her history. The French had for the moment cowed the Continent into a passive acceptance of their mastery. The opportunity was now at hand to concentrate the whole weight of the armed forces of France against the stubborn Islanders. An enormous army was organised and concentrated at the Channel ports for the invasion of England. At the crest of his hopes Napoleon had himself crowned by the Pope as Emperor of the French. One thing alone was lacking to his designs—command of the sea. It was essential to obtain naval control of the Channel before embarking upon such an enterprise. As before and since in her history, the Royal Navy alone seemed to stand between the Island and national destruction.

In May 1803 Nelson had returned to the Mediterranean to resume command of his fleet. Here the fate of his country might be decided. It was his task to contain the French fleet in Toulon and stop it from raiding Sicily and the Eastern Mediterranean, or sailing into the Atlantic, whence it might lift the blockade of Rochefort and Brest, force the Channel, and co-operate with the armada from Boulogne. Nelson was well aware of the grim significance of the moment, and all his brilliance as a commander was employed on creating a first-class machine. He was not even superior in numbers to the main French fleet in Toulon harbour. Under such circumstances a literal hemming in of the French was impossible. Nelson's burning desire was to lure them out and fight them. Annihilation was his policy. Twice in the course of two years the French attempted a sortie, but retired. Throughout this time Nelson never set foot on shore.

Nelson was lying in wait off the Sardinian coastline in April 1805 when news reached him that Villeneuve was at sea, having slipped out of Toulon on the dark night of March 30, sailing, as Nelson did not yet know, in a westerly direction. The fox was out and the chase began. Nelson, picking up scattered reports from frigates and merchantmen, pieced together the French design. All his qualities were now displayed to the full. Out of perplexing, obscure, and conflicting reports he had fathomed the French plan. Therefore on May 11 Nelson made the momentous decision to sail westwards himself. He had ten ships of the line to follow seventeen of the enemy. The

Toulon was the main naval base in southern France.

Villeneuve was the admiral commanding the French fleet.

passage was uneventful. In stately procession at an aver-
age rate of five and a half knots the English pursued their
quarry, and a game of hide-and-seek followed among the
West Indian islands. His arrival alarmed the French admiral, who was promptly out again in the Atlantic by
June 8, heading east. On the 12th Nelson lay off Antigua,
where Villeneuve had lain only four days earlier. He again
had to make a crucial decision. Was he right in believing
that the French were making for Europe?

Nelson reached Cadiz on July 18. There he found
Admiral Collingwood on guard, but no sign of the enemy.
Realising that Villeneuve must have gone north, Nelson
replenished his fleet in Morocco and sailed for home
waters on the 23rd. On the same day Napoleon arrived
at Boulogne. The crisis was at hand and the outlying
squadrons of the Royal Navy instinctively gathered at the
mouth of the Channel for the defence of the Island. On
the next day Nelson arrived, bringing the main fleet up to
a total of nearly forty ships of the line. Thus was the sea-
barrier concentrated against the French. Nelson went on
alone with his flagship, the *Victory*, to Portsmouth. In the
following days the campaign reached its climax. Then
Villeneuve, having edged out into the Atlantic, changed

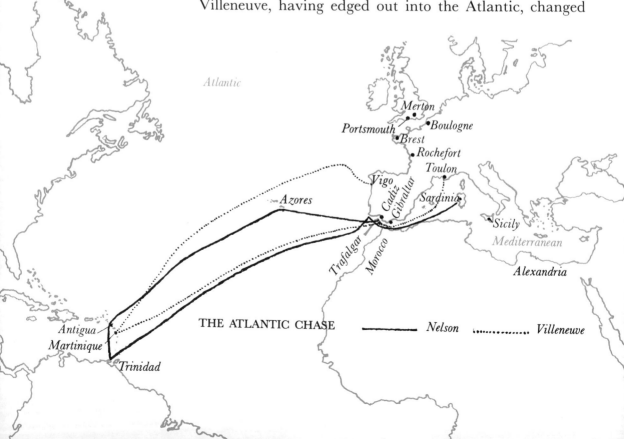

THE ATLANTIC CHASE ———— Nelson ·············· Villeneuve

his mind. Well aware of the shortcomings of his ill-trained fleet, desperately short of supplies, and with many sick on board, he abandoned the great venture and was speeding south to Cadiz. The threat of invasion was over.

Early in September dispatches reached London telling that Villeneuve had gone south. Nelson, summoned from his home at Merton, was at once ordered to resume his command. "I hold myself ready to go forth whenever I am desired," he wrote, "although God knows I want rest." Amid scenes of enthusiasm he rejoined the *Victory* at Portsmouth and sailed on September 15. All England realised that her fate now lay in the hands of this frail man. A fortnight later he joined the fleet off Cadiz. "We have only one great object in view," he wrote to Collingwood, "that of annihilating our enemies." His object was to starve the enemy fleet, now concentrated in Cadiz harbour, and force it out into the open sea and to battle. His energy and inspiration roused the spirit of his captains to the highest pitch. To them he outlined a new and daring plan of battle. He intended to ignore the Admiralty's "Fighting Instructions." To gain a decisive victory, he was resolved to abandon the old formal line of battle, running parallel to the enemy's fleet. He would break Villeneuve's line, when it came out of port, by sailing at right angles boldly into it with two main divisions. After his conference with his captains Nelson wrote, "All approved. It was new, it was singular, it was simple. It must succeed." In a mood of intense exhilaration the fleet prepared for the ordeal ahead. On the morning of October 19 a frigate signalled to Nelson's flagship, "Enemy ships are coming out of port." On receiving these messages Nelson led his fleet to the southeast to cut off the enemy from the Straits and force them to fight in the open sea. The enemy turned northwards on seeing the advancing squadrons, and Nelson pressed on with every sail set. The clumsy seamanship of his men convinced Villeneuve that flight was impossible, and he hove to in a long sagging line to await Nelson's attack. The English admiral turned to one of his officers. "They have put a good face on it, but I will give them such a dressing as they have never had before." Nelson

Nelson's health had been weak since boyhood. In earlier battles he had lost his right eye in 1794 and his right arm in 1797.

Napoleon menaces the world with his early arrogance. Within an ocean pattern are various scenes in Nelson's life: the loss of his eye at Calvi and of his arm at Tenerife; his major battles; his four ships before the Victory. At Copenhagen he defies a flag order to retreat, holding his spyglass before his bad eye so that he cannot see

ADMIRAL HORATIO NELSON

the signal. The white space indicates a temporary peace between England and France during which Nelson spends much of his time at home. Finally comes the battle of Trafalgar where Nelson is carried wounded below deck and dies just after the great victory is announced to him.

went down to his cabin to compose a prayer. "May the Great God whom I worship grant to my country, and for the benefit of Europe in general, a great and glorious Victory. . . . For, myself, I commit my life to Him who made me, and may His blessing light upon my endeavours for serving my country faithfully." The fleets were drawing nearer and nearer. Another signal was run up upon the *Victory,* "England expects every man will do his duty." When Collingwood saw the flutter he remarked testily, "I wish Nelson would stop signalling, as we all know well enough what we have to do," but when the message was reported to him cheers broke out from the ships in his line. A deathly silence fell upon the fleet as the ships drew nearer. Each captain marked down his adversary, and within a few minutes the two English columns thundered into action. The roar of broadsides, the crashing of masts, the rattle of musketry at point-blank range rent the air. The *Victory* smashed through between Villeneuve's flagship, the *Bucentaure,* and the *Redoutable.* The three ships remained locked together, raking each other with broadsides. Nelson was pacing as if on parade on his quarterdeck when at 1.15 P.M. he was shot from the mast-head of the *Redoutable* by a bullet in the shoulder. His backbone was broken, and he was carried below amid the thunder of the *Victory's* guns.

In the log of the *Victory* occurs the passage, "Partial firing continued until 4.30, when a victory having been reported to the right Hon. Lord Viscount Nelson, K.B. and Commander-in-Chief, he then died of his wound."

The victory was complete and final. The British Fleet, under her most superb commander, like him had done its duty.

DUKE OF WELLINGTON

1769-1852

NAPOLEON

THE CONVENTION OF CINTRA

THE PENINSULAR CAMPAIGN

THE BATTLE OF THE NATIONS

"FAREWELL, PORTUGAL!"

THE HUNDRED DAYS

FIELD-MARSHAL BLÜCHER

THE BATTLE OF WATERLOO

WHEN VILLENEUVE that summer of 1805 failed to break through into the Channel Napoleon made a sudden change of plan. The campaign that followed wrecked Pitt's hopes and schemes. In the month of Trafalgar the Austrian General Mack surrendered at Ulm. Austria and Russia were broken at the Battle of Austerlitz. Napoleon's star had once more triumphed, and for England all was to do again. About this time the Prime Minister gave audience to a young general home from India. In forthright terms this officer noted his opinion of Pitt. "The fault of his character," he wrote, "is being too sanguine. . . . He conceives a project and then imagines it is done." This severe but not inaccurate judgment was formed by one who was to have many dealings with the armies of the French Emperor. His name was Arthur Wellesley, later Duke of Wellington.

Napoleon, insatiable of power, and seeking always to break England and her intangible blockade, resolved to seize the Spanish crown. The character of the warfare darkened. In Germany and Italy and elsewhere there had been pillage and rough deeds, but the armies had given quarter and the inhabitants had remained spectators. Now, in Spain, the French troops found as they marched the corpses of their stragglers and wounded, often horribly mutilated, sometimes bearing signs of torture. It was with a chill that they realised they were at grips with a foe who, though incompetent in a set battle, neither gave nor sought mercy. Moreover, this foe lay everywhere. Napoleon felt in every nerve and fibre the tremor which ran through Europe and jarred the foundations of his Imperial throne. Here and now he was strong enough to quit Spain; his power would still have been enormous; but he feared to retreat from a false and dangerous position. He must move, like all dictators, from one triumph to another. This country, which he had expected to incorporate in his Empire by a personal arrangement with a feeble Government, by a trick, by a trap, without bloodshed or expense, suddenly became his main military problem. He resolved to conquer.

But meanwhile the English had decided to send an

126

army to the peninsula to aid the Spanish insurgents. In July 1808 this small British army consisting of 30,000 well-equipped men disembarked north of Lisbon. At the head of the first troops to land appeared Sir Arthur Wellesley, whose conduct of the war in India had been distinguished. He was the younger brother of the Governor-General of India. He was a member of Parliament and of the Tory administration, and actually held office at this time as Chief Secretary to the Lord-Lieutenant of Ireland. He did not wait for the rest of the army, but immediately took the field. The French columns of assault were broken by the reserved fire of the "thin red line," which now began to attract attention. Junot retreated upon Lisbon.

Andoche Junot was the General in command of the French troops.

Sir Arthur Wellesley was superseded in the moment of victory by the arrival of Sir Harry Burrard, who later in the same day made over his command to Sir Hew Dalrymple. Wellesley's wish to cut Junot's line of retreat was frustrated by his seniors. But the French commander now offered to negotiate. The Convention of Cintra was signed, and punctiliously executed by the British. Junot and twenty-six thousand Frenchmen were landed from British transports at Rochefort. Wellesley in dudgeon remarked to his officers, "We can now go and shoot red-legged partridges." There was a loud and not unnatural outcry in England at Junot's being freed. A military court of inquiry in London exonerated the three commanders, but only one of them was ever employed again.

He was the one that mattered:

> Sir Arthur and Sir Harry,
> Sir Harry and Sir Hew,
> Sing cock-a-doodle doodle,
>   doodle-doodle-doo.
>
> Sir Arthur was a fighting cock,
> But of the other two
> Sing doodle-doodle-doodle,
>   doodle-doodle-doo.

History has endorsed Byron's line, "Britannia sickens, Cintra! at thy name."

George Gordon, Lord Byron, was a famous English poet.

A new English general of high quality succeeded the commanders involved in the Convention of Cintra. Sir John Moore advanced from Lisbon through Salamanca to Valladolid. He had been lured by promises of powerful Spanish assistance, and he tried by running great risks to turn Spanish hopes into reality. His daring thrust cut or threatened the communications of all the French armies, and immediately prevented any French action in the south of Spain or against Portugal. But Napoleon, watching from Madrid, saw him a prey.

Moore's countrymen may well do him justice. By daring, skill, and luck he ruptured Napoleon's winter campaign and drew the Emperor and his finest army into the least important part of Spain, thus affording protection and time for movements to get on foot in all the rest of the Peninsula. He had escaped Napoleon's amazing forward spring and clutch. He died like Wolfe and Nelson, in the hour of victory. His army re-embarked unmolested. His campaign had restored the military reputation of Britain, which had suffered increasing eclipse since the days of Chatham; he had prepared the way for a new figure, destined to lead the armies of Europe upon the decisive field.

General James Wolfe in 1759 stormed the Heights of Abraham to take Quebec from the French and to die on the field.

In April of 1809 Arthur Wellesley was re-appointed to take command in Lisbon. He was to spend the next five years in the Peninsula, and return to London in triumph by way of the capital of France.

Wellesley resigned his seat in Parliament and his office as Chief Secretary, and reached Lisbon before the end of the month. He decided first to clear Portugal. With very small loss he compelled the French to withdraw into the mountainous regions of the north. Wellesley now resolved to penetrate into the centre of Spain along the valley of the Tagus. His campaigns were successful but costly. He could no longer place any reliance upon the co-operation of his Spanish allies. They engaged the enemy in their own free way, which was certainly not his. Like Sir John Moore before him, he had run enormous risks, and had been saved only by the narrowest of margins. He withdrew unmolested along the Tagus back to Portugal. Not only had he established the reputation of a highly skilful and determined general, but the fighting quality of the British had made a profound impression upon the French. In England there was unwonted satisfaction. Sir Arthur Wellesley was raised to the peerage as Viscount Wellington, and, in spite of Whig opposition, was granted a pension of £2,000 a year for three years. Nelson was gone; Pitt was gone; but here at last was someone to replace them.

These were testing years for Wellington. He commanded Britain's sole remaining army on the continent of Europe. Failure would have been disastrous to Britain, and to the patriots in Spain and Portugal; it would also have liberated large numbers of French troops for the reinforcement of Napoleon's ventures elsewhere. We can only speculate upon what further triumphs the Emperor might have enjoyed, even perhaps in Russia, but for the steady drain on his resources caused by Wellington's presence in the Peninsula. All this was not lost upon the English commander. But for the time being caution must be his policy. "As this is the last army England has," he drily wrote, "we must take care of it." The British commander had eager critics, even within his own army, who could not appreciate the wisdom of his steadily developing strategy. Wellington himself was unperturbed by cries for haste. Nothing could shake him, and he kept his own counsel. He was determined to secure behind him a broad base and reliable communications before he ventured into the recesses of Spain. Wellington had gauged precisely the size and scope of the task before him. A war of manoeuvre unfolded in 1811 within the Spanish frontiers, and both the French armies blocking his advance were separately met and defeated. Of one of them Wellington admitted, "If Boney had been there we should have been beaten." But Napoleon was not there. He was enmeshed in diplomacy and preparations for war elsewhere. Besides, he had just solemnised his second marriage. The Corsican's bride was a daughter of the proud house of Habsburg, the Archduchess Marie Louise. She gave him a long-desired son and heir, but little happiness.

In 1812 Wellington fell back once more on the Portuguese frontier. In the year's campaign he had shattered one French army and enabled the whole of Southern Spain to be freed from the French. But meanwhile heavier shadows from the East were falling upon Napoleon's Empire. It was the winter of the retreat from Moscow. Defence, retreat, and winter—on these resources the Russian high command relied. Napoleon had studied the amazing Russian campaigns of the great Swede, King Charles XII. He thought he had profited by his reading. In the twentieth century another more ruthless dictator was to study Napoleon's errors. He too thought he had marked the lesson. Russia undeceived them both.

The other "ruthless dictator" was, of course, Sir Winston's chief opponent, Adolf Hitler.

On December 5 Napoleon abandoned the remnant of his armies on the Russian frontier and set out by sleigh for Paris. Whatever salvaging could be done he left to his Marshals. For himself he was insensible of disaster. He still put trust in his Star. If he had failed to extend his Empire to the East, he could yet perceive it in the West. By tremendous efforts he would raise new forces and fight again. In the spring of 1813 he once more took the field. Coalitions were formed, backed by the finances of Britain. Napoleon was offered the chance of an honourable peace. Thinking that fate could be reversed by genius in battle, he rejected it. A series of gigantic engagements were fought in Saxony and Silesia. At last in the three-day battle of

Leipzig in October all Napoleon's foes closed in upon him. Nearly half a million men were involved on each side. In this Battle of the Nations Napoleon was overwhelmed and driven westwards to the frontiers of France. The Allies gathered on the borders of their enemy for the first time since 1793. The great Revolutionary and Imperial adventure was drawing to a close.

*   *   *

On the southern front Wellington's achievement surpassed all expectations. Issuing from his frontier bastions in May 1813, he flourished his cocked hat. "Farewell, Portugal!" he exclaimed. "I shall never see you again." Nor did he.

Tenaciously Wellington had pursued his purpose of reducing, as he put it, "the power and influence of the grand disturber of Europe." By the spring of 1814 he was on French soil and had occupied Bordeaux. In early April he sought out and defeated his old antagonist, Soult, at Toulouse.

Nicolas Jean de Dieu Soult was one of Napoleon's celebrated Marshals.

For Napoleon the end had already come. He was never more brilliant in manoeuvre than during his brief campaign of 1814, but at the end of March Marshal Marmont, defending Paris, gave up and surrendered the capital. On April 3 Napoleon abdicated and retired to the island of Elba. The long, remorseless tides of war rolled back, and at the Congress of Vienna the Powers prepared for the diplomatic struggle of the peace.

In the New Year of 1815 peace reigned in Europe and in America. In Paris a stout, elderly, easy-going Bourbon sat on the throne of France, oblivious of the mistakes made by his relations, advisers, and followers. His royalist supporters, more royal than their King, were trying the patience of his new-found subjects. The French people, still dreaming of Imperial glories, were ripe for another adventure. A sharp and sudden shock was needed to recall them to their unity of purpose. It came from a familiar quarter.

Napoleon had for nine months been sovereign of Elba. The former master of the Continent now looked out upon

a shrunken island domain. He kept about him the apparatus of Imperial dignity. He played cards with his
mother and cheated according to his recognised custom.
He entertained his favourite sister and his faithful Polish
mistress. Only his wife, the Empress Marie Louise, and
their son were missing. The Austrian Government took
care to keep them both in Vienna. The Empress showed
no sign of wishing to break her parole. Family Habsburg
loyalty meant more to her than her husband.

As the months went by close observers became sure
that Napoleon was biding his time. He was keeping a
watch on events in France and Italy. Through spies he
was in touch with many currents of opinion. He perceived
that the restored Bourbons could not command the loyalty
of the French. Besides, they had failed to pay him the annual pension stipulated in the treaty of peace. This act
of pettiness persuaded Napoleon that he was absolved
from honouring the treaty's terms. On Sunday night, the
26th of February Napoleon took lightning advantage. He
slipped out of harbour in his brig, attended by a small
train of lesser vessels. At the head of a thousand men he
set sail for France. On March 1 he landed near Antibes.

The drama of the Hundred Days had begun, and a
bloodless march to Paris ensued. Royalist armies sent
to stop the intruder melted away or went over to him.
Marshal Ney, "the Bravest of the Brave," who had taken
service under the Bourbons, boasted that he would bring
his former master back to Paris in an iron cage. He found
that he could not resist the Emperor's call; he joined
Napoleon. Other Marshals who had turned their coats now
turned them again. Within eighteen days of his landing
Napoleon was installed in the capital. The Bourbons ran
for cover. The Emperor proclaimed his peaceful intentions,
and at once started shaping his army. He showed all his
usual energy. He abounded in self-confidence. But the
flashing military judgment of earlier years was dimmed.
The gastric ulcer from which he had long suffered caused
him intermittent pain.

There was no time to lose. Wellington recommended
the immediate transport of an army to the Netherlands,

to form bases for a march on Paris and prepare for a clash upon the frontiers. Within a month of the escape from Elba Wellington took up his command at Brussels. As the summer drew near Wellington assembled a mixed force of eighty-three thousand men, of whom about a third were British. He bluntly cursed, as was his habit, the quality of his untried troops, while bending all his endeavours to train and transform them.

*   *   *

Napoleon could not afford to waste a day. Nor did he do so. His two main enemies stood on his north-eastern frontier within a few days' march of his capital. He must strike immediately at his gathering foes. The moral value of victory would be overwhelming, and the prestige of the British Government would be shaken. But where would he land his first blow? Wellington waited patiently in Brussels for a sign of the Emperor's intention. He and his great opponent were to cross swords for the first time. They were both in their forty-sixth year. Quietly on June 15 Napoleon struck at the hinge of the Allied armies. The capture of Brussels would be a great forward stride. Possession of a capital city was always a lure for him, and a source of strength.

Liaison between the British and Prussians was mysteriously defective and hours passed before the news reached Wellington. It seemed as though there was no detailed plan of co-operation between the Allied commanders. Military intelligence, as so often at the neap of events, was confusing and contradictory. There were no British troops on the Waterloo-Charleroi road, which was held thinly by a Dutch-Belgian division. On the night of the 15th, while the French armies massed to destroy the Prussians, the Duchess of Richmond gave a ball in Brussels in honour of the Allied officers. Wellington graced the occasion with his presence. He knew the value of preserving a bold, unruffled face. Amid the dancing he reflected on the belated news which had reached him. At all costs contact must be maintained with the Prussians and the French advance upon Brussels held.

SPAIN

PORTUGAL

PENINSULAR WAR — 1808 - 1813

" BRITANNIA SICKENS, CINTRA! AT THY NAME"

" AS THIS IS THE LAST ARMY ENGLAND HAS, WE MUST TAKE CARE OF IT "

" FAREWELL, PORTUGAL, I SHALL NEVER SEE YOU AGAIN "

RM

THE DUKE OF WELLINGTON

Wellington is shown against a background map of Portugal and western Spain where he fought his famous Peninsular campaign and gradually gained ascendancy over the French. Leaving it behind, he rides toward the

final test in northern Europe. Napoleon is now broken by the disastrous retreat from Moscow and is exiled in Elba until he escapes for his last great battle and final defeat at Waterloo.

For the French everything depended upon beating the Prussians before forcing Wellington north-westwards to the coast. Napoleon had in mind the vision of a shattered British army grimly awaiting transports for home in the Flemish ports. But the tardiness and sureness of Wellington's movements deceived him. Napoleon had gained the advantage at the opening of the campaign but he seems to have departed from his original plan. The crisis was at hand.

There seems no doubt that in the opening days Wellington had been surprised. As he confessed at the time, Napoleon's movements had "humbugged" him. Years later, when he read French accounts, he declared with his habitual frankness, "Damn them, I beat them, and if I was surprised, if I did place myself in so foolish a position, they were the greater fools for not knowing how to take advantage of my faults."

Wellington himself had inspected this Belgian countryside in the autumn of 1814. He had noted the advantages of the ridge at Waterloo. So had the great Duke of Marlborough a century earlier, when his Dutch allies had prevented him from engaging Marshal Villeroi there. His un-

Churchill is referring to the great Battle of Ramilles in 1706, when his ancestor, the Duke of Marlborough, defeated the French under Marshal Villeroi.

fought battle was now to unroll. Throughout the night of the 16th and 17th a carefully screened retreat began, and by morning the Waterloo position, a line of defence such as Wellington had already tested in the Peninsula, was occupied. Upon the French must be forced the onus of a frontal attack. Wellington knew that time was playing against his adversary. Swift results must be achieved by Napoleon if he was to establish himself again in France. Meanwhile Napoleon, furious to hear of Wellington's skilful withdrawal, pounded in his carriage down the Brussels road with his advance-guard in a desperate attempt to entrap the British rear. The mercy of a violent storm slowed up progress. The English cavalry galloped for safety through the thunder and torrential rain. An angry scene took place upon the meeting of Napoleon and Ney, who was greeted with the words from the Emperor, "You have ruined France!" As Napoleon reached the ridge of Waterloo and saw the British already in their positions he realised how complete had been their escape.

Late in the morning of the 18th of June the French attacked both flanks of the Allied position. Napoleon promised his staff they would sleep that night in Brussels. And to Soult, who raised some demur, he said, "You think Wellington a great general because he beat you. I tell you this will be a picnic." The battle swayed backwards and forwards upon the grass slopes. No visible decision was achieved. Napoleon, looking through his glasses at the awful *mêlée*, exclaimed, "Will the English never show their backs?" "I fear," replied Soult, "they will be cut to pieces first."

The long-awaited moment to counter-attack had come. Wellington had been in the forefront of danger all day. On his chestnut, Copenhagen, he had galloped everywhere, issuing brusque orders, gruffly encouraging his men. Now he rode along his much-battered line and ordered the advance. "Go on, go on!" he shouted. "They will not stand!" His cavalry swept from the ridge and sabred the French army into a disorganised mass of stragglers. Ney, beside himself with rage, a broken sword in his hand, staggered shouting in vain from one band to another. It was too late. Wellington handed over the pursuit to the Prussians. In agony of soul Napoleon followed the road back to Paris.

Late that night Blücher and Wellington met and embraced. *"Mein lieber Kamerad,"* said the old German Field-Marshal, who knew not a word of English, *"quelle affaire!,"* which was about all the French he could command. This brief greeting was greatly to Wellington's laconic taste. It was a story he delighted to repeat in later years when recalling his memories of Waterloo. The Duke rode back to Brussels. The day had been almost too much even for a man of iron. The whole weight of responsibility had fallen on him. Only the power and example of his own personality had kept his motley force together. The strain had been barely tolerable. "By God!" as he justly said, "I don't think it would have been done if I had not been there." As he took tea and toast and had the casualty lists read to him he broke down and wept.

Napoleon had reached his capital three days after the battle. He had a momentary surge of hope. He would fight again in France a campaign like that of 1814. But no one shared his optimism. The grand officials of the Empire, who owed him their positions and fortunes, had had enough. On June 22 he abdicated and retired to Malmaison. On July 6 Wellington entered the capital. Two days after the Allies' arrival Louis XVIII appeared. His second restoration was largely of Wellington's making. Wellington had no high regard for the Bourbons, but he was convinced that France under their shaky rule would no longer have the power to disturb the peace of Europe. Louis XVIII was no *Grand Monarque* and could never aspire to become one. Wellington, like many great soldiers when victory is complete, looked forward to an age of tranquillity. Laurels and bays had been won; it was time to cultivate the olive.

Malmaison was a hamlet a few miles west of Paris noted for its castle, the residence of Napoleon's former Empress Josephine.

Napoleon left Malmaison at the end of June. He made for the Biscay coast, narrowly evading capture on the way by the Prussians. Had they taken him they would have shot him. He had thoughts of sailing for America, and he ordered a set of travel books about the transatlantic continent. Perhaps a new Empire might be forged in Mexico, Peru, or Brazil. The alternative was to throw himself upon the mercy of his most inveterate foe. This is what happened. The Government, acting for the Allies, decided on exile in St. Helena, an island about the same size as Jersey, but very mountainous, and far away. Escape from it was impossible. On July 26 the Emperor sailed to his sunset in the South Atlantic. He never permitted himself to understand what had happened at Waterloo. The event was everybody's fault but his own. Six years of life in exile lay before him. He spent them with his small faithful retinue creating the Napoleonic legend of invincibility which was to have so powerful an effect on the France of the future. Wellington took command of the occupying army. For the next three years he was practically a Great European Power in himself. Much of the credit for the broad peace which Europe enjoyed after the fall of Napoleon was due to his robust common sense and shrewd judgment and in Wellington all men acknowledged the illustrious General who had met and beaten Napoleon.

The area of St. Helena is about 47 square miles. Jersey, southernmost of the Channel Islands, is 45 square miles.

ABRAHAM LINCOLN
1809-1865

ROBERT E. LEE
1807-1870

STEPHEN DOUGLAS

THE DRED SCOTT CASE

JEFFERSON DAVIS

GENERAL GEORGE McCLELLAN

THE EMANCIPATION PROCLAMATION

STONEWALL JACKSON

ULYSSES S. GRANT

APPOMATTOX COURT HOUSE

In the years following 1850 the prospects of the United States filled America with hope and Europe with envious admiration. Here democracy, shielded by the oceans and the Royal Navy from European dangers, founded upon English institutions and the Common Law, stimulated by the impulse of the French Revolution, seemed at last to have achieved both prosperity and power. In all material affairs the American people surpassed anything that history had known before.

Yet thoughtful men and travellers had for some time observed the approach of the convulsion which would grip not only the body but the soul of the United States. Of the three races who dwelt in North America, the Whites towered overwhelming and supreme. The Red Men, the original inhabitants, age-long product of the soil and climate, shrank back, pushed, exploited, but always disdainful, from the arms, and still more from the civilisation, of the transplanted European society by which they were ousted and eclipsed. The Black Men presented a problem, moral, social, economic, and political, the like of which had never before been known. It was said that both these races were downtrodden by White ascendancy as truly as animals are mastered, used, or exterminated by mankind. The proud Redskin was set upon his road to ruin by an excessive liberty. Almost all the four million Negroes were slaves.

It is almost impossible for us nowadays to understand how profoundly and inextricably Negro slavery was interwoven into the whole life, economy, and culture of the Southern states. But the North, once largely indifferent to the fate of slaves, had been converted by the 1850's to the cause of anti-slavery. The moral surge of the age stirred alike the New England states of the Atlantic shore and the powerful, swiftly growing population of the Middle West of the American Union. A gulf of sentiment and interest opened and widened between the Northern and Southern states. In the North many of the leaders, religious and secular, felt intensely that the whole future of the noble continent they had won lay under a curse.

The savage struggle between free-soil and slavery in

the Great Plains brought from the backwoods into national politics a new figure. Abraham Lincoln, a small-town lawyer from Springfield, Illinois, was stirred to the depths of his being by the passing of the Kansas-Nebraska Act. He had already served a term in Congress; now he stood for the Senate. He espoused the duty of opposing by the moral force of his personality the principle of slavery. "'A house divided against itself cannot stand.' I believe this Government cannot endure permanently half slave and half free. I do not expect the Union to be dissolved—I do not expect the house to fall—but I do expect it will cease to be divided. It will become all one thing or all the other." In a series of public debates and speeches Lincoln fought Douglas throughout the prairie towns of Illinois in the summer and autumn of 1858, and although he was beaten for the Senatorship he had already become a national figure. He had made slavery a moral and not a legal issue, and he had propounded the disruptive idea of overriding the Supreme Court's decision in the Dred Scott case and of outlawing slavery in the new territories.

Now came the fateful Presidential election of 1860. The Southern Senator Jefferson Davis demanded that the Northern states should repeal their Personal Liberty Laws and cease to interfere with the Fugitive Slave Law of 1850. Chief Justice Taney's decision of the Supreme Court must be obeyed. Slavery could not be prohibited by the Federal Government in the Territories of the United States. Rather, Davis demanded, the Federal Government should protect slavery in those areas. Against this, Abraham Lincoln unfolded in magnificent orations, calm, massive, and magnanimous, the antislavery cause. Secession was not the issue, though everyone felt that the South would in fact secede if Lincoln won. Slavery was the dominating and all-absorbing topic. Lincoln and the Republicans wanted to reverse the Dred Scott decision, prohibit slavery in the Territories and confine it within its existing limits. On November 6, 1860 Lincoln was elected.

In spite of the great majority against breaking the Union, the state of South Carolina passed by a unanimous

The Kansas-Nebraska Act introduced the principle of "squatter sovereignty" or local option on the slavery question in territories as they became new states.

Stephen Douglas, the "little giant," was the presidential candidate of the Democratic Party in 1860.

When Dred Scott, a Missouri slave, sued for his freedom, he was sold to a citizen of another state. He then transferred his suit from the State to the Federal courts and the case came by appeal to the Supreme Court. Its decision in 1857 put Scott out of court on the ground that a slave could not be a citizen of the United States.

vote at Charleston its famous Ordinance of Secession, declaring that the Union of 1788 between South Carolina
and all other states, Northern and Southern alike, was dissolved. This precipitate and mortal act was hailed with
delirious enthusiasm. The cannons fired; the bells rang;
flags flew on every house. The streets were crowded with
cheering multitudes. The example of South Carolina was
followed by six other states. Delegates from these sovereign states, as they regarded themselves, organised a new
Confederacy, of which Jefferson Davis was chosen President. A new constitution, similar in almost all respects to
that of the United States, but founded explicitly upon
slavery, was proclaimed. A Confederate flag—the Stars
and Bars—was adopted.

Strenuous efforts at compromise were being made.
Many Northerners were prepared for the sake of peace to
give way to the South on the slavery issue. But Lincoln
was inflexible. He would not repudiate the platform on
which he had been elected. He could not countenance
the extension of slavery to the Territories. This was the
nub on which all turned. In this tense and tremendous
situation Abraham Lincoln was sworn President on March
4, 1861. Around him the structure of Federal Government
was falling to pieces. Officials and officers were every day
leaving for their home states in the South. Hands were
clasped between old comrades for the last time in friendship.

So far only the cotton states, or Lower South had
severed themselves from the Union. Seven more and above
all the noble and ancient Virginia, the Old Dominion, the
birthplace of Washington, the fountain of American tradition and inspiration, still hung in the balance. Lincoln
appealed for patience and conciliation. He disclaimed all
intention of invading the South. He announced that he
would not interfere with slavery in the Southern states.
He revived the common memories of the North and South,
which, like "mystic cords, stretch from every battlefield
and patriot grave to every living heart . . . over this broad
land." "In your hands," he exclaimed, "my dissatisfied
fellow-countrymen, and not in mine, is this momentous

issue of civil war. The Government will not assail you. You can have no conflict without yourselves being the aggressors. You have no oath registered in Heaven to destroy the Government, while I shall have the most solemn one to preserve and defend it."

On April 8 Lincoln informed the Governor of South Carolina of his intention to re-victual Major Anderson and his eighty-three men in Fort Sumter. Thereupon President Davis ordered General Beauregard to demand the immediate surrender of the fort. Vain parleys were held; but before dawn on April 12 the Confederate batteries opened a general bombardment. After two days Anderson and his handful of men, feeling that all had been done that honour and law required, marched out begrimed and half suffocated and were allowed to depart to the North. No blood had been shed, but the awful act of rebellion had occurred.

The cannonade at Fort Sumter resounded through the world. It roused and united the people of the North. All the free states stood together. Party divisions were effaced. Upon this surge and his own vehement resolve, Lincoln issued a proclamation calling for the militia of the Union to suppress combinations in seven states "too powerful to be suppressed by the ordinary course of judicial proceedings." Here, then, was the outbreak of the American Civil War.

*   *   *

Upon Lincoln's call to arms to coerce the seceding states Virginia made without hesitation the choice which she was so heroically to sustain. She would not fight on the issue of slavery, but stood firm on the constitutional ground that every state in the Union enjoyed sovereign rights. Virginia seceded from the Union and placed her entire military forces at the disposal of the Confederacy. This decided the conduct of one of the noblest Americans who ever lived, and one of the greatest captains known to the annals of war.

Robert E. Lee stood high in American life. His father had been a colonel in the Revolution. By his marriage with Miss Custis, a descendant of Mrs. George Washington, he became the master of Arlington, the house overlooking the national capital which George Custis, Washington's adopted son, "the child of Mount Vernon," as he was called, had built for himself a few miles from Washington's own home. A graduate of West Point, General Scott's Engineer Staff-Officer in the Mexican War, Lee had served for more than twenty-five years in the United States Army with distinction. His noble presence and gentle, kindly manner were sustained by religious faith and an exalted character. As the American scene darkened he weighed carefully, while commanding a regiment of cavalry on the Texan border, the course which duty and honour would require from him. He was opposed to slavery and thought that "secession would do no good," but he had been taught from childhood that his first allegiance was to the state of Virginia. Summoned to Washington during March 1861, he had thus expressed himself to an intimate Northern friend: "If Virginia stands by the old Union, so will I. But if she secedes (though I do not believe in secession as a constitutional right, nor that there is sufficient cause for revolution), then I will still follow my native state with my sword, and if need be with my life."

He reached the capital in the fevered days of March, and General Scott, his old chief, wrestled earnestly with him in a three hours' interview. By Lincoln's authority he was offered the chief command of the great Union army now being raised. He declined at once, and when a day later Virginia seceded he resigned his commission, bade farewell for ever to his home at Arlington, and in the deepest sorrow boarded the train for Richmond. Here he was immediately offered the chief command of all the military and naval forces of Virginia. He had resigned his United States commission on the Saturday, and on the Monday following he accepted his new task. Some of those who saw him in these tragic weeks, when sometimes his eyes filled with tears, emotion which he never showed after the gain or loss of great battles, have written about his inward struggle. But there was no struggle; he never hesitated. The choice was for the state of Virginia. He deplored that choice; he foresaw its consequences with bitter grief; but for himself he had no doubts at the time, nor ever after regret or remorse.

In the task of preparing for war the Southern President had advantages over his rival. A West-Pointer, he had fought in the Mexican War; he had afterwards been Secretary of War. He had an inside knowledge of the officer corps, and could make the best use of the material at his disposal. Not only did he select with a few exceptions the right men, but he supported them in adversity. The principal Confederate Generals who were in command at the beginning of the war, if not killed, were still in command at its end.

Lincoln, on the other hand, was without military experience; his profession of the law had not brought him in contact with Army officers. His appointments were too often made on purely political grounds. He was too ready, especially at first, to yield to the popular clamour which demanded the recall of an unsuccessful general. Few, having failed once, were given a second chance. After each defeat a change was made in the command of the Army of the Potomac. None of the Generals in command of Federal armies at the end of the war had held high commands at the beginning. The survivors were very good, but the Federal cause was the poorer for the loss of those who had fallen by the way. Others, fearing the President in the rear more than the foe in front, had been too nervous to fight their best. Lincoln's vacillations are a classic instance of the dangers of civilian interference with generals in the field. If these two Presidents had let McClellan and Lee fight the quarrel out between them as they thought best the end would have been the same, but the war would have been less muddled, much shorter, and less bloody.

Upon Virginia joining the Confederacy Jefferson Davis made Richmond the Southern capital. It was within a hundred miles of Washington. Between Richmond and the enemy flowed in successive barriers the broad outlets of the Potomac and the Rappahannock, with its tributary the Rapidan. Here, then, upon this advanced battleground,

Sir Winston was trained at Sandhurst, England's foremost military academy, and was for many years a professional soldier.

George McClellan was at this time the General in command of the Union armies.

rather than in the interior, must the Confederacy maintain itself or fall. Thus the two capitals stood like queens at chess upon adjoining squares, and, sustained by their combinations of covering pieces, they endured four years of grim play within a single move of capture.

War had never reached such an intensity of moral and physical forces focused upon decisive points as in the campaigns of 1862. The number of battles that were fought and their desperate, bloody character far surpassed any events in which Napoleon ever moved. From June 1, when Lee was given the command, the Army of Northern Virginia fought seven ferocious battles—the Seven Days, Cedar Run, the Second Manassas, South Mountain, Harpers Ferry, the Antietam, and later Fredericksburg—in as many months. Lee very rarely had three-quarters, and several times only half, the strength of his opponents. These brave Northerners were certainly hampered by a woeful political direction, but, on the other side, the Confederates were short of weapons, ammunition, food, equipment, clothes, and boots. It was even said that their line of march could be traced by the bloodstained footprints of unshod men. But the Army of Northern Virginia "carried the Confederacy on its bayonets" and made a struggle unsurpassed in history.

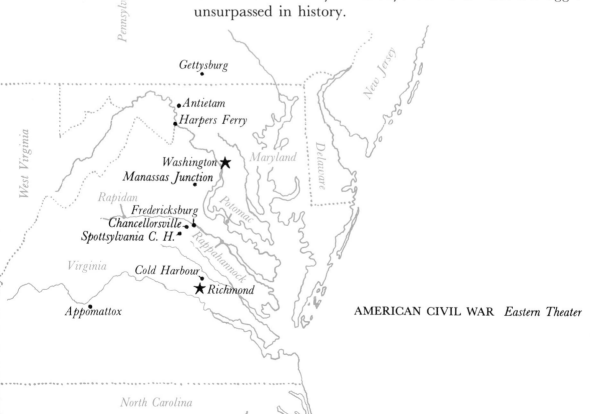

AMERICAN CIVIL WAR *Eastern Theater*

Lincoln had hoped for a signal victory. McCellan at the Antietam presented him with a partial though important success. But the President's faith in the Union cause was never dimmed by disappointments. He was much beset by anxieties, which led him to cross-examine his commanders as if he were still a prosecuting attorney. The Generals did not relish it. But Lincoln's popularity with the troops stood high. They put their trust in him. They could have no knowledge of the relentless political pressures in Washington to which he was subjected. They had a sense however of his natural resolution and generosity of character. He had to draw deeply on these qualities in his work at the White House. Through his office flowed a stream of politicians, newspaper editors, and other men of influence. Most of them clamoured for quick victory, with no conception of the hazards of war. Many of them cherished their own amateur plans of operation which they confidently urged upon their leader. Many of them too had favourite Generals for whom they canvassed. Lincoln treated all his visitors with patience and firmness. His homely humour stood him in good stead. A sense of irony helped to lighten his burdens. In tense moments a dry joke relieved his feelings. At the same time his spirit was sustained by a deepening belief in Providence. When the toll of war rose steeply and plans went wrong he appealed for strength in his inmost thoughts to a power higher than man's. Strength was certainly given him. It is sometimes necessary at the summit of authority to bear with the intrigues of disloyal colleagues, to remain calm when others panic, and to withstand misguided popular outcries. All this Lincoln did. Personal troubles also befell him. One of his beloved sons died in the White House. Mrs. Lincoln, though devoted to her husband, had a taste for extravagance and for politics which sometimes gave rise to wounding comment. As the war drew on Lincoln became more and more gaunt and the furrows on his cheeks and brow bit deep. Fortitude was written on his countenance.

The Antietam and the withdrawal of Lee into Virginia gave the President an opportunity to take a momentous step. He proclaimed the emancipation of all the slaves in

the insurgent states. The impression produced in France
and Britain by Lee's spirited and resolute operations, with
their successive great battles, either victorious or drawn,
made the Washington Cabinet fearful of mediation, to be
followed, if rejected, by recognition of the Confederacy.
The North was discouraged by disastrous and futile losses
and by the sense of being out-generalled. Recruitment fell
off and desertion was rife. Many urged peace, and others
asked whether the Union was worthy of this slaughter, if
slavery was to be maintained. By casting down this final
challenge and raising the war to the level of a moral crusade Lincoln hoped to rally British public opinion to the
Union cause and raise a new enthusiasm among his own
fellow-countrymen.

It was a move he had long considered. Even since the
beginning of the war the Radicals had been pressing for
the total abolition of slavery. Lincoln had misgivings about
the effects on the slave-owning states of the border which
had remained loyal. "My paramount object is to save the
Union, and is not either to save or to destroy slavery. . . .
What I do about slavery and the coloured race, I do because it helps to save the Union; and what I forbear, I
forbear because I do not believe it would help to save the
Union." Meanwhile he was meditating on the timing of
his Proclamation and on the constitutional difficulties that
stood in the way. He felt his Proclamation could be legally
justified only as a military measure, issued in virtue of
his office as Commander-in-Chief of the Army and Navy.
When the Proclamation was published, with effect from
January 1st, 1863, it therefore applied only to the rebel
states. There it only came into force as the Federal armies
advanced and the war assumed an implacable character,
offering to the South no alternative but subjugation. Many
Northerners thought that the President had gone too far,
others that he had not gone far enough. Great, judicious,
and well-considered steps are thus sometimes at first received with public incomprehension.

*   *   *

Chancellorsville was the finest battle which Lee and

Jackson fought together. Their combination had become perfect. "Such an executive officer," said Lee, "the sun never shone on. Straight as the needle to the pole, he advances to the execution of my purpose." "I would follow General Lee blindfold" is a remark attributed to Jackson. Now all was over. "Could I have directed events," wrote Lee, ascribing the glory to his stricken comrade, "I should have chosen for the good of the country to be disabled in your stead." The conduct of this battle illustrates again the agile, flexible grasp which Lee had of war, and how great commanders seem to move their armies from place to place as if they were doing no more than riding their own horses. But no one knew Jackson's plan, and he was now unconscious. Thus on small agate points do the balances of the world turn.

Jackson lingered for a week. His arm was amputated. Pneumonia supervened. On the 10th he was told to prepare for death, to which he consented with surprise and fortitude. "Very good, very good; it is all right." Finally, after some hours, quietly and clearly: "Let us cross over the river and rest under the shade of the trees." His loss was a mortal blow to Lee and to the cause of the South.

*   *   *

Lee at Gettysburg no more than Napoleon at Waterloo could win dominance. The victorious stormers were killed or captured; the rest walked home across the corpses which encumbered the plain amid a remorseless artillery fire. Less than a third came back. Lee met them on his horse Traveller with the only explanation which they would not accept, "It is all my fault." The Battle of Gettysburg was at an end. Twenty-three thousand Federals and over twenty thousand Confederates had been smitten by lead or steel. As after the Antietam, Lee confronted his foe on the morrow and offered to fight again. But no one knew better that it was decisive. With every personal resource he gathered up his army. An immense wagon train of wounded were jolted, springless, over sixteen miles of crumpled road. On the night of the 4th Lee began his retreat. Meade let him go. After a cruel night march, Lee was safe on the

Thomas Jonathan Jackson, commonly called Stonewall Jackson, was Lee's second in command. Just before this, he had been fatally wounded by his own sentries when returning on horseback from a nighttime reconnaissance.

General George Gordon Meade was in command of the Union armies at Gettysburg.

ABRAHAM LINCOLN

The log cabin where Lincoln was born is symbolic of his humble beginnings. Above his thoughtful figure rises the spectre of slavery which leads to the clash of the Civil War. The Union side is blue, commanded at the end by Grant, and the Confederate side is grey, under Lee. The bloody interval between them draws to an end

GENERAL ULYSSES S. GRANT.   GENERAL ROBERT E. LEE

at Appomattox. The figures in mourning represent the general public after the assassination, and the funeral train makes its sad way into the distance.

other side of the river. He carried with him his wounded
and his prisoners. He had lost only two guns, and the war.

We must now turn to the West where great battles
were fought and many fell. From the West, the eventual
thrust came which split and devastated the South. But its
importance in 1862 and 1863 lay chiefly in the advance
of Grant to the supreme unified command of the Union
armies. The Federal General, Henry W. Halleck, who commanded the Western Department was a model of caution.
Fortunately among his generals there was a retired Regu-
lar officer, Ulysses S. Grant, who since the Mexican War
had lived in obscurity, working for a time in his father's
leather store in Illinois. Grant proposed a winter advance
up the Tennessee River and an attack upon Fort Henry.
Halleck approved. Grant made the advance, and the advance made Grant.

The Washington Government now began to lean heavily upon General Ulysses Grant. His faults and weaknesses
were apparent; but so also was his stature. On the Union
side, baffled, bewildered, disappointed, weary of bloodshed
and expense, Grant now began to loom vast and solid
through a red fog. Victory had followed him from Fort
Donelson to Vicksburg. Here were large rebel surrenders—
troops, cannon, territory. Who else could show the like?

By the end of 1863 all illusions had vanished. The
South knew they had lost the war, and would be conquered
and flattened. It is one of the enduring glories of the American nation that this made no difference to the Confederate
resistance. In the North, where success was certain, they
could afford to have bitter division. On the beaten side the
 departure of hope left only the resolve to perish arms in
hand. Better the complete destruction of the whole generation and the devastation of their enormous land, better
that every farm should be burned, every city bombarded,
every fighting man killed, than that history should record
that they had yielded. Any man can be trampled down by
superior force, and death, in whatever shape it comes, is
only death, which comes to all. It might seem incredible
when we survey the military consequences of 1863 that the
torments of war should have been prolonged through the

whole of 1864 and into 1865. "Kill us if you can; destroy all we have," cried the South. "As you will," replied the steadfast majority of the North.

On March 9 President Lincoln appointed Ulysses Grant to the command of all the armies of the United States, raising him to the rank of Lieutenant-General. At last on the Northern side there was unity of command, and a general capable of exercising it. Grant's plan was brutal and simple. It was summed up in the word "Attrition." In intense fighting and exchange of lives weight of numbers would prevail.

With the approach of spring Grant, having launched the Union Army, came to grips with Lee on the old battle-grounds of the Rappahannock and the Rapidan, where the traces of Chancellorsville remained and memories of "Stonewall" Jackson brooded. This was called the Battle of Spottsylvania Court House, in which the Federal armies suffered a loss of over eighteen thousand men, or double of that of their opponents. Undeterred by the slaughter, Grant repeated his movement to the left, and prolonged heavy fighting followed. Grant, for all the courage of his men, could never turn Lee's right flank, and Lee and his devoted soldiers could never overcome odds of two to one. They could only inflict death and wounds in proportion to their numbers. According to Grant's war-thought, this process, though costly, had only to be continued long enough to procure the desired result. "I propose to fight it out on this line," he wrote to Halleck at Washington, "if it takes all summer." These concepts, although they eventually gained their purpose, must be regarded as the negation of generalship. They were none the less a deadly form of war.

At Cold Harbour the Federal Commander-in-Chief hurled his army through the blasted, undulating woodland against the haggard, half-starved, but elated Confederate lines. But the result of the day ended Grant's tactics of unflinching butchery. After seven thousand brave blue-coated soldiers had fallen in an hour or so the troops refused to renew the assault. More is expected of the high command than determination in thrusting men to their doom. The

Union dead and wounded lay between the lines; the dead soon began to stink in the broiling sun, the living screamed for water. But Grant failed to secure a truce for burial and mercy. It was not till the third day after the battle that upon a letter from Lee, saying he would gladly accord it if asked, formal request was made, and for a few hours the firing ceased. During the World Wars through which we have lived no such indulgences were allowed, and numbers dwarfing the scale of the American Civil War perished in "no-man's-land," in long, helpless agony where they fell. But in that comparatively civilised and refined epoch in America, Cold Harbour was deemed a horror almost beyond words.

But the most important conflict of 1864 was fought with votes. It was astonishing that in the height of ruthless civil war all the process of election should be rigidly maintained. Lincoln's first term was expiring, and he must now submit himself to the popular vote of such parts of the American Union as were under his control. Nothing shows the strength of the institutions which he defended better than this incongruous episode. Lincoln's political foes, gazing upon him, did not know vigour when they saw it. These were hard conditions under which to wage a war to the death. The awful slaughters to which Grant had led the Army of the Potomac and the prolonged stalemate outside Richmond made a sinister impression upon the North. But the capture of Atlanta, and a descent by Admiral Farragut upon the harbour of Mobile, the last Confederate open port, both gave that surge of encouragement which party men know how to use. Four million citizens voted in November 1864, and Lincoln was chosen by a majority of only four hundred thousand. Narrow indeed was the margin of mass support by which his policy of the remorseless coercion of the Southern states to reincorporation was carried.

On Sunday, April 2, President Davis sat in his pew in the church at Richmond. A messenger came up the aisle. "General Lee requests immediate evacuation." Southward then must the Confederate Government wander. There were still some hundreds of miles in which they exercised authority. Nothing crumbled, no one deserted; all had to be overpowered, man by man and yard by yard. Lee had still a plan. He would march swiftly south from Richmond, unite with Johnston, break Sherman, and then turn again to meet Grant and the immense Army of the Potomac. But all this was for honour, and mercifully that final agony was spared. Lee, disengaging himself from Richmond, was pursued by more than three times his numbers, and Sheridan, with a cavalry corps, lapped around his line of retreat and broke in upon his trains. When there were no more half-rations of green corn and roots to give to the soldiers, and they were beset on three sides, Grant ventured to appeal to Lee to recognise that his position was hopeless. Lee bowed to physical necessity. He rode on Traveller to Appomattox Court House to learn what terms would be offered. Grant wrote them out in a few sentences. The officers and men of the Army of Northern Virginia must surrender their arms and return on parole to their homes, not to be molested while they observed the laws of the United States. Lee's officers were to keep their swords. Food would be provided from the Union wagons. Grant added, "Your men must keep their horses and mules. They will need them for the spring ploughing." This was the greatest day in the career of General Grant, and stands high in the story of the United States. The Army of Northern Virginia, which so long had "carried the Confederacy on its bayonets," surrendered, twenty-seven thousand strong; and a fortnight later, despite the protests of President Davis, Johnston accepted from Sherman terms similar to those granted to Lee. Davis himself was captured by a cavalry squadron. The armed resistance of the Southern states was thus entirely subdued.

Lincoln had entered Richmond with Grant, and on his return to Washington learned of Lee's surrender. Conqueror and master, he towered above all others, and four years of assured power seemed to lie before him. By his constancy under many varied strains and amid problems to which his training gave him no key he had saved the Union with steel and flame. His thoughts were bent upon healing his country's wounds. For this he possessed all the qualities of

General Joseph E. Johnston was in command of the Confederate army opposing the Union General William Tecumseh Sherman, who was invading the deep South.

spirit and wisdom, and wielded besides incomparable authority. To those who spoke of hanging Jefferson Davis he replied, "Judge not that ye be not judged." On April 11 he proclaimed the need of a broad and generous temper and urged the conciliation of the vanquished. At Cabinet on the 14th he spoke of Lee and other Confederate leaders with kindness, and pointed to the paths of forgiveness and goodwill. But that very night as he sat in his box at Ford's Theatre a fanatical actor, one of a murder gang, stole in from behind and shot him through the head. The miscreant leapt on the stage, exclaiming, *"Sic semper tyrannis,"* and although his ankle was broken through his spur catching an American flag he managed to escape to Virginia, where he was hunted down and shot to death in a barn. Seward, Secretary of State, was also stabbed at his home, though not fatally, as part of the same plot.

Lincoln died next day, without regaining consciousness, and with him vanished the only protector of the prostrate South. Others might try to emulate his magnanimity; none but he could control the bitter political hatreds which were rife. The assassin's bullet had wrought more evil to the United States than all the Confederate cannonade. Even in their fury the Northerners made no reprisals upon the Southern chiefs. Jefferson Davis and a few others were, indeed, confined in fortresses for some time, but afterwards all were suffered to dwell in peace. But the death of Lincoln deprived the Union of the guiding hand which alone could have solved the problems of reconstruction and added to the triumph of armies those lasting victories which are gained over the hearts of men.

Who overcomes
By force hath overcome but half his foe.

 Thus ended the great American Civil War, which must upon the whole be considered the noblest and least avoidable of all the great mass-conflicts of which till then there was record.

QUEEN VICTORIA

1819-1901

PALMERSTON

MELBOURNE

PRINCE ALBERT

THE CRYSTAL PALACE

THE CRIMEAN WAR

FLORENCE NIGHTINGALE

GLADSTONE

DISRAELI

THE BOER WAR

The sons of George III were George IV; Frederick, who died in 1827; William IV; Edward, father of Victoria; Ernest, King of Hanover, and Adolphus.

IN 1837 KING WILLIAM IV died. Humorous, tactless, pleasant, and unrespected, he had played his part in lowering esteem for the monarchy, and indeed the vices and eccentricities of the sons of George III had by this time almost destroyed its hold upon the hearts of the people. An assault on the institution which had played so great a part in the history of England appeared imminent, and there seemed few to defend it. The new sovereign was a maiden of eighteen. She had been brought up by a dutiful mother, who was shocked at the language and habits of the royal uncles, and had secluded her in Kensington Palace from both the Court and the nation. Her education was supervised by a German governess, with occasional examinations by Church dignitaries, and a correspondence course on her future duties with her maternal uncle, King Leopold of Belgium. The country knew nothing of either her character or her virtues. "Few people," wrote Palmerston, "have had opportunities of forming a correct judgment of the Princess; but I incline to think she will turn out to be a remarkable person, and gifted with a great deal of strength of character." He was right. On the eve of her accession the new Queen wrote in her diary: "Since it has pleased Providence to place me in this station, I shall do my utmost to fulfil my duty towards my country; I am very young, and perhaps in many, though not in all things, inexperienced, but I am sure that very few have more real good will and more real desire to do what is fit and right than I have." It was a promise she was spaciously to fulfil.

By the time Queen Victoria came to the throne the Whigs had shot their bolt. In 1839 Melbourne offered to resign, but for another two years Victoria kept him in office. His charm had captured her affections. He imparted to her much of his wisdom on men and affairs, without burdening her with his scepticism, and she refused to be separated from her beloved Prime Minister. In February of the following year a new figure entered upon the British scene. The Queen married her cousin, Prince Albert of Saxe-Coburg. The Prince was an upright, conscientious man with far-ranging interests and high ideals. He and the Queen enjoyed for twenty-one years, until his early death,

The Whigs and Tories were the two main political parties at the beginning of Victoria's reign. The Liberals and Conservatives were the two principal parties at the end.

158

a happy family life, which held up an example much in accord with the desires of her subjects. After the excesses of George IV and his brothers the dignity and repute of the monarchy stood in need of restoration, and this was Victoria and Albert's achievement. At first the Prince found his presence in England resented by the political magnates of the time. They would not let him take a seat in the House of Lords, they cut down his annual allowance, and he was not granted even the title of Prince Consort until 1857. Nevertheless the patronage which he earnestly extended to science, industry, and the arts, and to good causes of many kinds, gradually won him a wide measure of public respect. As permanent adviser to the Queen, on all issues laid before her, he played a scrupulous, disinterested part. Wise counsels from his uncle, King Leopold, and his former tutor, Baron Stockmar, taught him the role and duties of a constitutional sovereign. Eventually the party leaders in England learnt to value his advice, especially on foreign affairs, though they did not always pay heed to it. The Queen was a woman of strong mind, who had begun her reign as a vehement partisan of the Whigs. Under Albert's influence she came to perceive that in public at least she must be impartial and place her trust in whichever Minister could command a majority in the House of Commons. This did not prevent her from entertaining vivid likes and dislikes for her chief servants, to which she gave vigorous expression in private letters. Together the Queen and the Prince set a new standard for the conduct of monarchy which has ever since been honourably observed.

While party affairs at Westminster dwelt gently in flux, Europe succumbed to an anguished spasm. In February 1848 the French monarchy fell. The rule of King Louis Philippe had given prosperity to France, or at least to her middle classes, but it had never been accepted by the adherents of the elder Bourbon line, and it appealed neither to staunch Republicans nor to the Bonapartists, who were still dazzled by the remembered glories of the Empire. A few days of rioting sufficed to eject Louis Philippe, and by the end of the year a Bonaparte had been elected Presi-

Prime Ministers under Victoria:
Viscount Melbourne, 1835–1841
Sir Robert Peel, 1841–1846
Lord John Russell, 1846–1852
Earl of Derby, 1852
Earl of Aberdeen, 1852–1855
Viscount Palmerston, 1855–1858
Earl of Derby, 1858–1859
Viscount Palmerston, 1859–1865
Lord John Russell, 1865–1866
Earl of Derby, 1866–1868
Benjamin Disraeli, 1868
William Gladstone, 1868–1874
Benjamin Disraeli, 1874–1880
William Gladstone, 1880–1885
Marquis of Salisbury, 1885–1886
William Gladstone, 1886
Marquis of Salisbury, 1886–1892
William Gladstone, 1892–1894
Earl of Rosebery, 1894–1895
Marquis of Salisbury, 1895–1902

dent of France by an overwhelming majority. Thus, after half a lifetime spent in plotting, exile, and obscurity, Prince Louis Napoleon, nephew of the great Emperor, came to power. He owed his position to the name he bore, to the ineptitude of his rivals, and to the fondness of the French for constitutional experiment. For more than twenty years this amiable, dreamy figure was to play a striking and not always ineffective part upon the European scene.

In the same year Thomas Babington Macaulay, who had been a Minister of the Crown and served the Government of India in high office, published the first volumes of his *History of England*. This great work, with all its prejudiced opinions and errors of fact, provided the historical background for the sense of progress which was now inspiring Victorian Britain. Macaulay set out to show that the story of England since the Whig Revolution of 1688 was one of perpetual and limitless advance. In his opening chapter he wrote: "The history of our own country in the last hundred and sixty years is eminently the history of physical, moral, and intellectual improvement." This was a heartening note, much appreciated by contemporary readers. Optimism reigned throughout the land. An even more shining future, Macaulay implied, lay before the United Kingdom. So indeed it did. His views were widely shared, and were soon given form in the Great Exhibition of British achievement which justly gratified the nation.

Prince Albert sponsored the idea. There had already been small exhibitions of manufactures, in which he had taken an interest. In 1849, after opening the new Albert Dock in Liverpool, the Prince had been so much impressed by the surging vigour of British industry, and its maritime cause and consequence, that he adopted with enthusiasm a plan for an exhibition on a far larger scale than had ever been seen before. It would display to the country and the world the progress achieved in every field. It would also be international, proclaiming the benefits of free trade between nations and looking forward to the universal peace which it was then supposed must inevitably result from the unhampered traffic in goods. Few people foresaw the war with Russia that was soon to break out.

For two years, against considerable opposition, the Prince headed a committee to further his project. In 1851 the Great Exhibition was opened in Hyde Park. Nineteen acres were devoted to the principal building, the Crystal Palace, designed by an expert glasshouse gardener, Joseph Paxton. Housing most of the exhibits, and enclosing whole trees within its glass and iron structure, it was to be the marvel of the decade. In spite of prophecies of failure, the Exhibition was a triumphant success. Over a million people a month visited it during the six months of its opening. Nearly fourteen thousand exhibits of industrial skill and craft were shown, of which half were British. The Prince was vindicated, and the large profit made by the organisers was invested and put to learned and educational purposes. Queen Victoria described the opening day as "one of the greatest and most glorious in our lives." Her feelings were prompted by her delight that Prince Albert should have confounded his critics, ever ready to accuse him of meddling in national affairs, but there was more to it than that. The Queen paid many visits to the Crystal Palace, where her presence aroused in the scores of thousands of subjects with whom she mingled a deep loyalty and a sense of national pride. Never had the Throne been so firmly grounded in the affections of the people. Prosperity, however unevenly its blessings fell, gave Britain a self-assurance that seemed worth more than social legislation and further reform. From mills and mines and factories flowed the wealth that was making life easier for the country. And this the country recognised.

*   *   *

Foreign affairs and the threat of war now began to darken the scene. The Turks had troubled the statesmen of Europe for many years and their military empire, which for three centuries had dominated the Eastern world from the Persian Gulf to Budapest, and from the Caspian to Algiers, seemed now on the edge of disruption and collapse. What then would become of its vast territories? To whom would fall the wide, fertile Turkish provinces in Europe and Asia? The urgency and imminence of such questions were sharpened by the evident determination of Russia to seize the Danubian lands, Constantinople, and the Black Sea. England could not ignore the threat: the shadow of Russia, already a formidable Asiatic Power, appeared to be creeping over India. By 1853, the Russian attitude had become so menacing that the Cabinet ordered the British Fleet to the Dardanelles. Napoleon III, eager for British approval and support, agreed to provide a French squadron.

The English started the conquest of India about 1750 and completed it in about one hundred years. In 1877 Victoria was proclaimed Empress of India. In 1945 the country was granted independence.

In February 1854, Nicholas recalled his ambassadors from London and Paris, and at the end of March the Crimean War began, with France and Britain as the allies of Turkey.

At Balaclava in October the British cavalry distinguished themselves by two astonishing charges against overwhelming odds. The second of these was the celebrated charge of the Light Brigade, in which 673 horsemen, led by Lord Cardigan, rode up the valley under heavy fire, imperturbably, as if taking part in a review, to attack the Russian batteries. They captured the guns, but only a third of the brigade answered the first muster after the charge. Lord Cardigan calmly returned to the yacht on which he lived, had a bath, dined, drank a bottle of champagne, and went to bed. His brigade had performed an inspiring feat of gallantry. But it was due, like much else in this war, to the blunders of commanders. Lord Raglan's orders had been badly expressed and were misunderstood by his subordinates. The Light Brigade had charged the wrong guns.

With one exception few of the leading figures emerged from the Crimean War with enhanced reputations. Miss Florence Nightingale had been sent out in an official capacity by the War Minister. She arrived at Scutari on the day before the Battle of Inkerman, and there organised the first base hospital of modern times. With few nurses and scanty equipment she reduced the death-rate at Scutari from 42 per hundred to 22 per thousand men. Her influence and example were far-reaching. The Red Cross movement, which started with the Geneva Convention of 1864, was the outcome of her work, as were great administrative reforms in civilian hospitals. In an age of proud

and domineering men she gave the women of the nineteenth century a new status, which revolutionised the social life of the country, and even made them want to vote.
Miss Nightingale herself felt that "there are evils which
press much more hardly on women than the want of suffrage." Lack of education was one, and she favoured better girls' schools and the founding of women's colleges. To
these objects she devoted her attention, and by her efforts
half the Queen's subjects were encouraged to enter the
realms of higher thought.

Palmerston, though now in his seventies, presided over
the English scene. Not long after the signing of peace with
Russia the English were confronted with another emergency
which also arose in the East, but this time in India where
suddenly there occurred a disturbing outbreak against
British rule. The Indian Mutiny made, in some respects, a
more lasting impact on England than the Crimean War.
It paved the way for Empire. After it was over Britain
gradually and consciously became a world-wide Imperial
Power.

The scale of the Indian Mutiny should not be exagger-
ated. Three-quarters of the troops remained loyal; barely
a third of British territory was affected; there had been
risings and revolts among the soldiery before; the brunt of
the outbreak was suppressed in the space of a few weeks.
It was in no sense a national movement, or, as some later
Indian writers have suggested, a patriotic struggle for freedom or a war of independence. The idea and ideal of the
inhabitants of the sub-continent forming a single people
and state was not to emerge for many years. But terrible
atrocities had been committed by both sides. From now on
there was an increasing gulf between the rulers and the
ruled. The easy-going ways of the eighteenth century were
gone for ever, and so were the missionary fervour and re-
forming zeal of the early Victorians and their predecessors.
British administration became detached, impartial, effi-
cient. Great progress was made and many material benefits were secured. The frontiers were guarded and the
peace was kept. *Suttee,* the burning of widows, *Thugee,* the
strangling of travellers by fanatics who deemed it a reli-

gious duty, and female infanticide were suppressed. Starvation was subdued. The population vastly increased. The Indian army, revived and reorganised, was to play a glorious part on Britain's side in two world wars. Nevertheless the atrocities and reprisals of the blood-stained months of the Mutiny left an enduring and bitter mark in the memory of both countries.

While these events unrolled in India the political scene in England remained confused. Religious preoccupations were probably more widespread and deeply felt than at any time since the days of Cromwell. But thinking men were also disturbed by a new theory, long foreshadowed in the work of scientists, the theory of evolution. It was given classic expression in *The Origin of Species,* published by Charles Darwin in 1859. This book provoked doubt and perplexity among those who could no longer take literally the Biblical account of creation. But the theory of evolution, and its emphasis on the survival of the fittest in the history of life upon the globe, was a powerful adjunct to mid-Victorian optimism. It lent fresh force to the belief in the forward march of mankind.

In home politics meanwhile a sublime complacency enveloped the Government. Palmerston, like Melbourne before him, did not believe in too much legislation. Good-humour and common sense distinguished him. This practical outlook found no favour among the younger and more thrusting Members of the House of Commons. Disraeli, chafing on the Opposition benches, vented his scorn and irritation on this last of the eighteenth-century politicians. Disraeli had become the leader of his party in the House of Commons. His struggle for power was hard and uphill. A Jew at the head of a phalanx of country gentlemen was an unusual sight in English politics.

In 1865, in his eighty-first year Palmerston died. "Gladstone," he declared in his last days, "will soon have it all his own way, and whenever he gets my place we shall have strange doings." The old Whig was right. The eighteenth century died with him. The later Victorian age demanded a new leader, and at long last he had arrived. When Gladstone next appeared before his electors he opened his speech by saying, "At last, my friends, I am come among you, and I am come among you unmuzzled." In 1868 Disraeli was at last Prime Minister—as he put it "at the top of the greasy pole." He had to hold a General Election. The new voters gave their overwhelming support to his opponents, and Gladstone, who had become leader of the Liberal Party, formed the strongest administration that England had seen since the days of Peel.

We now enter upon a long, connected, and progressive period in British history—the Prime Ministerships of Gladstone and Disraeli. These two great Parliamentarians in alternation ruled the land from 1868 to 1885. For nearly twenty years no one effectively disputed their leadership, and until Disraeli died in 1881 the political scene was dominated by a personal duel on a grand scale. Both men were at the height of their powers, and their skill and oratory in debate gripped and focused public attention on the proceedings of the House of Commons. Every thrust and parry was discussed throughout the country. What gave the conflict its edge and produced a deep-rooted antagonism was their utter dissimilarity in character and temperament. "Posterity will do justice to that unprincipled maniac, Gladstone," wrote Disraeli, in private. Gladstone's judgment on his rival was no less sharp. His doctrine was "false, but the man more false than his doctrine." Thus they faced each other across the dispatch-boxes of the House of Commons: Gladstone's commanding voice, his hawk-like eyes, his great power to move the emotions, against Disraeli's romantic air and polished, flexible eloquence.

Nothing created more bitterness between the two than Gladstone's conviction that Disraeli had captured the Queen for the Conservative Party and endangered the Constitution by an unscrupulous use of his personal charm. When Gladstone became Prime Minister Victoria was still in mourning and semi-retirement for Prince Albert, who had died in 1861. She deeply resented his attempts to bring the monarchy back into public life, attempts which culminated in a well-intentioned scheme to make her eldest son the Viceroy of Ireland. Gladstone, though always respectful, was incapable of infusing any kind of warmth

THE CRYSTAL PALACE

GLADSTONE

THE CRIMEAN WAR—1854-1856

PRINCE ALBERT

FLORENCE NIGHTINGALE

The Prince Consort, Albert, stands against the background of the Crystal Palace which he promoted and which became his outstanding success. Below is a scene from the Crimean War, where Florence Nightingale ministers to the sick and wounded troops. Gladstone and Disraeli conduct their great debates in the House of Commons,

DISRAELI   QUEEN VICTORIA

a parliamentary climax in the reign of Victoria. Later, the Boer War breaks out. But, serenely presiding over her whole epoch, Victoria sits as the "grandmother of Europe."

into his relationship with her. She once said, according to report, that he addressed her like a public meeting. Disraeli did not make the same mistake. "The principles of the English Constitution," he declared, "do not contemplate the absence of personal influence on the part of the Sovereign; and, if they did, the principles of human nature would prevent the fulfillment of such a theory." He wrote to the Queen constantly. He wooed her from the loneliness and apathy which engulfed her after Albert's death, and flattered her desire to share in the formulation of policy. Victoria found this irresistible. She complained that Gladstone, when in office, never told her anything. She was not friendly to her Liberal Governments; she disliked Gladstone and detested the growing Radicalism of his party. But in fact little harm was done; Gladstone was careful to keep the person of the Queen out of political discussion and none of their disagreements was known to the public. He grumbled that "The Queen is enough to kill any man," but he served her patiently, if not with understanding. In any case the development of popular Government based on popular elections was bound to diminish the personal power of the Crown. In spite of her occasional leanings, Victoria remained a constitutional monarch.

It was not immediately perceived how deep a change was wrought in English politics by the long controversy over Home Rule for Ireland. The Home Rule Bill had at last been introduced into the Commons on April 8, 1886, by Gladstone in a speech which lasted for three and a half hours. He put the case for Home Rule as one of justice for Ireland and freedom for her people. It was an impressive performance, outstanding even in Gladstone's dazzling Parliamentary career. But his sudden conversion to the new policy, his dependence upon the Irish vote for continuance in office, and the bitter memories of Irish crimes combined to deepen the fears and prejudices of his opponents. The emotions of race, religion, class, and economic interest all obscured the Liberal arguments which Gladstone used. Fire evoked fire. Gladstone's deep moral feeling found its answer on the other side, which believed him to be a hypocrite or worse. He had embarked on a sudden, destructive crusade. "And why?" asked Lord Randolph Churchill. "For this reason, and no other: to gratify the ambition of an old man in a hurry."

The Bill was defeated. Gladstone resigned and Salisbury took office. Gladstone died in 1898. His career had been the most noteworthy of the century, leaving behind innumerable marks on the pages of history. He was the greatest popular leader of his age, and he has hardly been equalled in his power to move the people on moral issues. He stands, too, in the very front rank of House of Commons figures. Few of his conceptions were unworthy. Gladstone's achievements, like his failures, were on the grand scale.

Lord Randolph Churchill, Sir Winston's father, was an eminent statesman of the time.

*   *   *

Salisbury's interest and that of a large section of public opinion lay in the world overseas, where the Imperialist movement was reaching its climax of exploration, conquest, and settlement. Livingstone, Stanley and other travellers had opened up the interior of darkest Africa. Their feats of exploration paved the way for the acquisition of colonies by the European powers. It was the most important achievement of the period that this partition of Africa was carried out peacefully. The credit is largely due to Salisbury. The key to Salisbury's success lay in his skilful handling of the innumerable complications that arose between the Powers in an age of intense national rivalries. He once said that "British policy is to drift lazily downstream, occasionally putting out a boat-hook to avoid a collision." No British Foreign Secretary has wielded his diplomatic boat-hook with greater dexterity.

Britain entered the twentieth century in the grip of war. She placed nearly half a million men in the field, the biggest force she had hitherto sent overseas throughout her history. The conflict in South Africa, which began as a small colonial campaign, soon called for a large-scale national effort. Of course there were vehement critics and dissentients, the pro-Boers, as they were derisively called. Nevertheless the general feeling in the country was staunchly

The Boers were the people of Dutch descent in South Africa. As first European settlers there, they resisted the advancing power of the British.

Imperialist. There was pride in the broad crimson stretches on the map of the globe which marked the span of the British Empire, and confidence in the Royal Navy's command of the Seven Seas. When British losses at Colenso came as a startling and heavy shock to the public Queen Victoria braced the nation in words which have become justly famous. "Please understand," she replied to Balfour, "that there is no one depressed in *this* house. We are not interested in the possibilities of defeat. They do not exist."

Arthur James Balfour was then leader of the House of Commons.

*   *   *

We have now reached in this account the end of the nineteenth century, and the modern world might reasonably have looked forward to a long period of peace and prosperity. Nearly a hundred years of peace and progress had carried Britain to the leadership of the world. She

THE **BRITISH EMPIRE** *of The Victorian Age*

had striven repeatedly for the maintenance of peace, at
any rate for herself, and progress and prosperity had been
continuous in all classes. The franchise had been extended
almost to the actuarial limit, and yet quiet and order
reigned. Conservative forces had shown that they could
ride the storm, and indeed that there was no great storm
between the domestic parties. As Wellington had remarked,
the English are "a very quiet people." This is especially
true when it is raining. The national horse had shown
that the reins could be thrown on his neck without leading to a furious gallop in this direction or that. Certainly
the dawn of the twentieth century seemed bright and calm
for those who lived within the unequalled bounds of the
British Empire, or sought shelter within its folds. There
was endless work to be done. None of the ancient inhibi-
tions obstructed the adventurous. If mistakes were made
they had been made before, and Britons could repair them
without serious consequences. To go forward gradually but
boldly seemed to be fully justified.

On January 22, 1901, Queen Victoria died. She lay at
Osborne, the country home in the Isle of Wight which
she and Prince Albert had designed and furnished fifty-
five years before. Nothing in its household arrangements
had been changed during the Queen's long widowhood.
She had determined to conduct her life according to the
pattern set by the Prince; nor did she waver from her
resolution. Nevertheless a great change had gradually over-
taken the monarchy. The Sovereign had become the symbol of Empire. At the Queen's Jubilees in 1887 and 1897
India and the colonies had been vividly represented in the
State celebrations. The Crown was providing the link between the growing family of nations and races which the
former Prime Minister, Lord Rosebery, had with foresight
christened the Commonwealth. Disraeli's vision and Chamberlain's enthusiasm had both contributed to the broadening Imperial theme. The Queen herself was seized with
the greatness of her role. She sent her sons and grandsons
on official tours of her ever-increasing dominions, where
they were heartily welcomed. Homage from a stream of
colonial dignitaries was received by her in England. She

appointed Indian servants to her household, and from
them learnt Hindustani. Thus she sought by every means
within her power to bind her diverse peoples together in
loyalty to the British Crown, and her endeavours chimed
with the Imperial spirit of the age. One of her last public
acts, when she was over eighty years of age, was to visit
Ireland. She had never believed in Irish Home Rule,
which seemed to her a danger to the unity of the Empire.
Prompted by a desire to recognise the gallantry of her
Irish soldiers in South Africa, she travelled to Dublin in
April 1900, wearing the shamrock on her bonnet and
jacket. Her Irish subjects, even the Nationalists among
them, gave her a rousing reception. In Ireland a fund of
goodwill still flowed for the Throne, on which English
Governments sadly failed to draw.

In England during the Queen's years of withdrawal
from the outward shows of public life there had once been
restiveness against the Crown, and professed republicans
had raised their voices. By the end of the century all this
had died away. High devotion to her royal task, domestic
virtues, evident sincerity of nature, a piercing and sometimes disconcerting truthfulness—all these qualities of the
Queen's had long impressed themselves upon the minds
of her subjects. In the mass they could have no knowledge
of how shrewd she was in political matters, nor of the wisdom she had accumulated in the course of her dealings
with many Ministers and innumerable crises. But they
justly caught a sense of a great presiding personage. Even
Ministers who in private often found her views impulsive
and partisan came to respect the watchful sense of duty
that always moved her. She represented staunchness and
continuity in British traditions, and as she grew in years
veneration clustered round her. When she died she had
reigned for nearly sixty-four years. Few of her subjects
could remember a time when she had not been their Sovereign. But all reflecting men and women could appreciate
the advance of British power and the progress of the British peoples that had taken place during the age to which
she gave her name. The Victorian Age closed in 1901, but
the sense of purpose and confidence which had inspired it
lived on through the ordeals to come.

WINSTON CHURCHILL

1874-1965

Winston Churchill is generally accepted and admired as the outstanding wartime leader of this century. Few can dispute this judgment, but one may ask, What made this man so great? And of course the answer is that he made himself so. Then we come to what he might have called the "nub of the matter" . . . how did he make himself so? If he were asked such a question, he would scornfully have refused to answer it. But he has answered it consciously and subconsciously many times in his writings and his speeches. So often has he given his answers that they lead in all their variety to a realization that this man was that rare occurrence in humankind—a combination of a wide range of talents and forces rather than a genius in any one field.

Let us look at these many facets, one by one, as he reveals them to us in his own words, and thus make the acquaintance of the greatest English-speaking hero of our times.

SCHOOLBOY

Winston Churchill was born
November 30, 1874,
in Blenheim Palace.
Lord Randolph Churchill
was his father. His mother was
an American, Jennie Jerome.

He was privately tutored
during his early years,
then went to Harrow
for his secondary education.

I did not do well in examinations. I would have liked to have been examined in history, poetry and writing essays. The examiners were partial to Latin and mathematics. I should have liked to be asked to say what I knew. They always tried to ask what I did not know. And their will prevailed.

I frequently heard the irreverent comment, "Why, he's last of all!" They all went on to learn Latin and Greek and splendid things like that. But I was taught English. We were considered such dunces that we could learn only English. Thus I got into my bones the essential structure of the ordinary English sentence—which is a noble thing.

It was thought incongruous that while I apparently stagnated in the lowest form, I should gain a prize open to the whole school for reciting to the Headmaster twelve hundred lines of Macaulay's *Lays of Ancient Rome* without making a single mistake. I also succeeded in passing the preliminary examination for the Army while still almost at the bottom of the school. This examination seemed to have called forth a very special effort on my part. I also had a piece of luck. We knew that among other questions we should be asked to draw from memory a map of some country or other. The night before I put the names of all the maps in the atlas into a hat and drew out New Zealand. I applied my good memory to the geography of that Dominion. Sure enough the first question in the paper was: "Draw a map of New Zealand."

I now embarked on a military career. This orientation was entirely due to my collection of soldiers. I had ultimately nearly fifteen hundred. They were all of one size, all British, and organised as an infantry division with a cavalry brigade.

The day came when my father himself paid a formal visit of inspection. All the troops were arranged in the correct formation of attack. He spent twenty minutes studying the scene—which was really impressive—with a keen eye and captivating smile. At the end he asked me if I would like to go into the Army. I thought it would be splendid to command an Army, so I said "Yes" at once: and immediately I was taken at my word.

At Sandhurst I think I was pretty well trained to sit and manage a horse. This is one of the most important things in the world. No one ever came to grief—except honourable grief—through riding horses. No hour of life is lost that is spent in the saddle. Young men have often been ruined through owning horses, or through backing horses, but never through riding them; unless of course they break their necks, which, taken at a gallop, is a very good death to die.

My course at Sandhurst soon came to an end. Instead of creeping in at the bottom, almost by charity, I passed out with honours, eighth in my batch of a hundred and fifty. I mention this because it shows that I could learn quickly enough the things that mattered.

PROFESSIONAL SOLDIER

Sandhurst, a parish in Berkshire, is the seat of the Royal Military College of England. Churchill graduated in 1895.

We three subalterns, pooling our resources, took a palatial bungalow, all pink and white, with heavy tiled roof and deep verandahs sustained by white plaster columns, wreathed in purple bougainvillea. It stood in a compound or grounds of perhaps two acres. We took over from the late occupant about a hundred and fifty splendid standard roses. We built a large tiled barn with mud walls, containing stabling for thirty horses and ponies. Our three butlers formed a triumvirate in which no internal dissensions ever appeared. We paid an equal contribution into the pot; and thus freed from mundane cares, devoted ourselves to the serious purpose of life.

This was expressed in one word—Polo.

Never in the history of Indian polo had a cavalry regiment from Southern India won the Inter-Regimental cup. I can hardly describe the sustained intensity of purpose with which we threw ourselves into this audacious and colossal undertaking. We knew it would take two or three years of sacrifice, contrivance and effort. But if all other diversions were put aside, we did not believe that success was beyond our compass. To this task then we settled down with complete absorption. I must not forget to say that there were of course also a great many military duties.

SPORTSMAN

In 1896 he was serving in India as a subaltern, a junior officer with less rank than a captain.

I was on the lawns of Goodwood in lovely weather and winning my money, when the revolt of the Pathan tribesmen of the Indian frontier began. I read in the newspapers that a Field Force of three brigades had been formed. Forthwith I telegraphed the General and took the train for Brindisi to catch the Indian Mail. I impressed Lord William Beresford into my cause. He reinforced my appeals to the General. He entertained me at the Marlborough Club before my train left Victoria. These Beresfords had a great air. They made one feel that the world and everyone in it were of fine consequence. I remember the manner in which he announced my purpose to a circle of club friends many years my seniors. "He goes to the East to-night—to the seat of war." "To the East"—the expression struck me. Most people would have said "He is going out to India;" but to that generation the East meant the gateway to the adventures and conquests of England. "To the Front?" they asked. Alas, I could only say I hoped so. I felt very important, but naturally observed a marked discretion.

I only just caught the train; but I caught it in the best of spirits.

One voyage to India is enough; the others are merely repletion. It was the hottest season of the year, and the Red Sea was stifling. But these physical discomforts were nothing beside my mental anxieties. I was giving up a whole fortnight's leave. At Brindisi no answer had come. It was sure to come at Aden. There I danced about from one foot to the other till the steward had distributed the last of the telegrams and left me forlorn. However, at Bombay was good news. The General's message was "Very difficult; no vacancies; come up as a correspondent; will try to fit you in."

I had first of all to obtain leave from my regiment at Bangalore. This meant a two days' journey by railway in the opposite direction to that in which my hopes were directed. Meanwhile I had been commissioned as war correspondent by the *Pioneer* newspaper, and my Mother had also arranged in England that my letters should be simultaneously published in the *Daily Telegraph,* for which that journal was willing to pay £5 a column. This was not much, considering that I had to pay all my own expenses. I carried these journalistic credentials when I presented in much anxiety the General's telegram to my commanding officer. But the Colonel was indulgent, and the fates were kind. Although the telegram was quite informal and unofficial, I was told that I could go and try my luck.

WRITER

I had meanwhile been working continuously upon *The River War*. This work was extending in scope. From being a mere chronicle of the Omdurman campaign, it grew backwards into what was almost a history of the ruin and rescue of the Soudan. I now planned a couple of fat volumes. I affected a combination of the styles of Macaulay and Gibbon, and I stuck in a bit of my own from time to time. I began to see that writing, especially narrative, was not only an affair of sentences, but of paragraphs. Just as the sentence contains one idea in all its fullness, so the paragraph should embrace a distinct episode; and as sentences should follow one another in harmonious sequence, so the paragraphs must fit on to one another like the automatic couplings of railway carriages. Chapterisation also began to dawn upon me. Finally the work must be surveyed as a whole and due proportion and strict order established from beginning to end.

Churchill had been in the cavalry, a lieutenant with the 4th Hussars in the Omdurman campaign in 1898.

The River War, his first book, was published in 1899.

It was great fun writing a book. One lived with it. It became a companion and there was never a moment when agreeable occupation was lacking. I have noticed in my life deep resemblances between many different kinds of things. Writing a book is not unlike building a house or planning a battle or painting a picture. The technique is different, the materials are different, but the principle is the same. The foundations have to be laid, the data assembled, and the premises must bear the weight of their conclusions. Ornaments or refinements may then be added. The whole when finished is only the successful presentation of a theme.

In all he wrote thirty-five volumes, his last work being A History of the English-Speaking Peoples, *completed in 1958. He was awarded the Nobel Prize for Literature in 1953.*

Until the year 1919, when I inherited unexpectedly a valuable property under the will of my long dead great-grandmother, I was entirely dependent upon my own exertions. During all these twenty years I maintained myself, and later on my family, without ever lacking anything necessary to health or enjoyment. I am proud of this, and I commend my example to my son, indeed to all my children.

OPPORTUNIST: ESCAPE FROM THE BOERS

He was taken prisoner by the Boers November 15, 1899, and made his escape the following December 12.

Now or never! I stood on a ledge, seized the top of the wall with my hands, and drew myself up. Twice I let myself down in sickly hesitation, and then with a third resolve scrambled up and over. I had one parting glimpse of the sentries still talking with their backs turned fifteen yards away. Then I lowered myself lightly down into the adjoining garden and crouched among the shrubs. I was free! The first step had been taken, and it was irrevocable. The gate which led into the road was only a few yards from another sentry. I said to myself, *"Toujours de l'audace,"* put my hat on my head, strode into the middle of the garden, walked past the windows of the house without any attempt at concealment, and so went through the gate and turned to the left. I passed the sentry at less than five yards. Most of them knew me by sight. Whether he looked at me or not I do not know, for I never turned my head. I restrained with the utmost difficulty an impulse to run. But after walking a hundred yards and hearing no challenge, I knew that the second obstacle had been surmounted. I was at large in Pretoria.

I walked on leisurely through the night, humming a tune and choosing the middle of the road. The streets were full of burghers, but they paid no attention to me. Gradually I reached the suburbs, and on a little bridge I sat down to reflect and consider. I was in the heart of the enemy's country. Nearly three hundred miles stretched between me and Delagoa Bay. My escape must be known at dawn. Pursuit would be immediate. Yet all exits were barred. The town was picketed, the country was patrolled, the trains were searched, the line was guarded. I wore a civilian brown flannel suit. I had seventy-five pounds in my pocket and four slabs of chocolate . . .

The noise and confusion of election crowds, the cant of phrase and formula, the burrowings of rival caucuses, fill with weariness, and even terror, persons of exquisite sensibility. It is easy for those who take no part in the public duties of citizenship to sniff disdainfully at the methods of modern politics. But it is a poor part to play. Amid the dust and brawling, with rude weapons and often unworthy champions, a real battle for real and precious objects is swaying to and fro. Better far the clamour of popular disputation, with all its most blatant accessories, hammering out from month to month and year to year the laboured progress of the common people in a work-a-day world, than the poetic tragedies and violences of chivalric ages.

POLITICIAN

It was an honour to take part in the deliberations of this famous assembly which for centuries had guided England through numberless perils forward on the path of empire. Though I had done nothing else for many months but address large audiences, it was with awe as well as eagerness that I braced myself for what I regarded as the supreme ordeal. I had only taken my seat for four days before I rose to address the House. The question in debate, which raised the main issue of the war, was one upon which I felt myself competent to argue or advise. I listened to counsel from many friendly quarters. Some said "It is too soon." Others said "It is your subject: do not miss the chance." I was warned against mere colourless platitude. But the best advice I got was "Don't be hurried; unfold your case. If you have anything to say, the House will listen."

The hour arrived. A sense of alarm and even despair crept across me. I repressed it with an inward gasp. I was up before I knew it. Courage returned. I got through all right. When I said "the Boers who are fighting in the field —*and if I were a Boer, I hope I should be fighting in the field*— . . ." I saw a ruffle upon the bench below me. But I could already see the shore at no great distance, and swam on vigorously till I could scramble up the beach, breathless physically, dripping metaphorically, but safe. Everyone

ORATOR IN THE HOUSE OF COMMONS

He was first elected to Parliament in 1900 and held many public offices throughout the rest of his life. His principal government posts were: Home Secretary, 1910–11 First Lord of the Admiralty, 1911–15 Secretary of War and Air Minister, 1918–21 Chancellor of the Exchequer, 1924–29 First Lord of the Admiralty, 1939 Prime Minister, First Lord of the Treasury, and Minister of Defense, 1940–45 Prime Minister, 1951–55 was very kind. The usual restoratives were applied, and I sat in a comfortable coma till I was strong enough to go home.

VISIONARY

He was Lieutenant Colonel in command of the 6th Royal Scots Fusiliers in France in 1916.

When I had joined the army in the previous November, I had written, at the invitation of the Commander-in-Chief, a paper embodying my ideas upon new methods of attacking the enemy. The Memorandum dealt with many secret projects in which I was deeply interested, including the scheme of using caterpillar vehicles (afterwards called "Tanks") in large numbers by surprise and in conjunction with smoke and other devices. The importance of this paper at the date at which it was written (3 December, 1915) can be judged from this extract:

"3 *Caterpillars.*—The cutting of the enemy's wire and the general domination of his firing-line can be effective by engines of this character. About seventy are now nearing completion in England, and should be inspected. None should be used until all can be used at once. They should be disposed secretly along the whole attacking front two or three hundred yards apart. Ten or fifteen minutes before the assault these engines should move forward over the best line of advance open, passing through or across our trenches at prepared points. They are capable of traversing any ordinary obstacle, ditch, breastwork, or trench. They carry two or three Maxims each, and can be fitted with flame-apparatus. Nothing but a direct hit from a field-gun will stop them. On reaching the enemy's wire they turn to the left or right and run down parallel to the enemy's trench, sweeping his parapet with their fire, and crushing and cutting the barbed wire in lanes and in a slightly serpentine course. While doing this the Caterpillars will be so close to the enemy's line that they will be immune from his artillery. Through the gaps thus made the shield-bearing infantry will advance.

"*If artillery is used to cut wire the direction and imminence of the attack is proclaimed days beforehand. But by this method the assault follows the wire-cutting almost immediately, i.e. before any reinforcements can be brought up by the enemy, or any special defensive measures taken.*"

Chance, Fortune, Luck, Destiny, Fate, Providence seem   FATALIST
to me only different ways of expressing the same thing,
to wit, that a man's own contribution to his life story is
continually dominated by an external superior power. If
anyone will look back over the course of even ten years'
experience, he will see what tiny incidents, utterly unim-
portant in themselves, have in fact governed the whole of
his fortunes and career. This is true of ordinary life. But
in war, which is an intense form of life, Chance casts all
veils and disguises and presents herself nakedly from moment to moment as the direct arbiter over all persons and
events. Starting out in the morning you leave your matches
behind you. Before you have gone a hundred yards, you
return to get them and thus miss the shell which arrived
for your express benefit from ten miles away, and are no
doubt shocked to find how nearly you missed the appointed rendezvous. You stay behind an extra half-minute
to pay some civility to a foreign officer who has unexpectedly presented himself; another man takes your place
in walking up the communication trench. Crash! He is no
more. You may walk to the right or to the left of a particular tree, and it makes the difference whether you rise
to command an Army Corps or are sent home crippled
or paralysed for life. You are walking up a duckboard
track; in front of you a shell is falling at half-minute intervals; you think it foolhardly to walk straight along the
track, especially as you notice that you will reach the dan-
ger-point almost on the tick of time; you deflect fifty yards
to the left; but the gun is traversing at the same time,
and meets you with a grim smile in the midst of your pre-
cautions.

If we look back on our past life we shall see that one
of its most usual experiences is that we have been helped by
our mistakes and injured by our most sagacious decisions.

Scenes of Churchill's early military career show his baptism of fire in Cuba and the charge of the 21st Lancers at Omdurman. As a journalist in the Boer War he is captured but makes a sensational escape. He is elected to the House of Commons. He becomes First Lord of the Admiralty on the outbreak of the First World War. Later

I EXPECT THAT THE BATTLE OF BRITAIN IS ABOUT TO BEGIN

"HITLER KNOWS THAT HE WILL HAVE TO BREAK US IN THIS ISLAND OR LOSE THE WAR."

"IF WE CAN STAND UP TO HIM, ALL EUROPE MAY BE FREE AND THE LIFE OF THE WORLD MAY MOVE FORWARD..."

"LET US THEREFORE BRACE OURSELVES TO OUR DUTIES, AND SO BEAR OURSELVES THAT, IF THE BRITISH EMPIRE AND ITS COMMONWEALTH LAST FOR A THOUSAND YEARS, MEN WILL STILL SAY, 'THIS WAS THEIR FINEST HOUR'

WORLD WAR II

ADOLF HITLER

CHARTWELL

INSTALLED KNIGHT COMPANION OF THE ORDER OF THE GARTER

1939   1945   1953

he becomes Chancellor of the Exchequer. The rise of Hitler in Germany leads to the Second World War. As Prime Minister he gives his famous "V for Victory" salute. He is made a Knight Companion of the Garter and, in later life, he retires to write and paint in his country home at Chartwell.

PHILOSOPHER   Let us be contented with what has happened to us and thankful for all we have been spared. Let us accept the natural order in which we move. Let us reconcile ourselves to the mysterious rhythm of our destinies, such as they must be in this world of space and time. Let us treasure our joys but not bewail our sorrows. The glory of light cannot exist without its shadows. Life is a whole, and good and ill must be accepted together. The journey has been enjoyable and well worth making—once.

It is above all things important that the moral philosophy and spiritual conceptions of men and nations should hold their own amid these formidable scientific evolutions. It would be much better to call a halt in material progress and discovery rather than to be mastered by our own apparatus and the forces which it directs. There are secrets too mysterious for man in his present state to know; secrets which once penetrated may be fatal to human happiness and glory. But the busy hands of the scientists are already fumbling with the keys of all the chambers hitherto forbidden to mankind. Without an equal growth of Mercy, Pity, Peace and Love, Science herself may destroy all that makes human life majestic and tolerable. There never was a time when the inherent virtue of human beings required more strong and confident expression in daily life.

COMMONER   Thus when all the trumpets sounded, every class and rank had something to give to the need of the State. Some gave their science and some their wealth, some gave their business energy and drive, and some their wonderful personal prowess, and some their patient strength or patient weakness. But none gave more, or gave more readily, than the common man or woman who had nothing but a precarious week's wages between them and poverty, and owned little more than the garments in which they stood upright. Their love and pride of country, their loyalty to the symbols with which they were familiar, their keen sense of right and wrong as they saw it, led them to outface and endure perils the like of which men had not known on earth.

Long live the forward march of the common people in all the lands towards their just and true inheritance, and towards the broader and fuller age.

We have sung of "the wonderful giants of old" but can anyone doubt that this generation is as good and as noble as any the nation has ever produced, and that its men and women can stand against all tests? Can any one doubt that this generation is in every way capable of carrying on the traditions of the nation and handing down its love of justice and liberty and its message undiminished and unimpaired?

When this war is won, as it surely will be, it must be one of our aims to work to establish a state of society where the advantages and privileges which hitherto have been enjoyed only by the few shall be far more widely shared by the many, and by the youth of the nation as a whole.

When the war was won, Churchill was offered many noble titles, but he chose always to remain a commoner and so accepted only a knighthood. He was made a Knight Companion of the Garter in 1953.

Where does the family start? It starts with a young man falling in love with a girl. No superior alternative has yet been found.

WIT

Young people should be careful in their reading, as old people in eating their food. They should not eat too much. They should chew it well.

If Hitler invaded Hell I would make at least a favourable reference to the Devil in the House of Commons.

I do not see any other way of realizing our hopes about world organisation in five or six days. Even the Almighty took seven.

I have never accepted what many people have kindly said, namely that I inspired the nation. Their will was resolute and remorseless, and as it proved, unconquerable. It was the nation and the race dwelling all round the globe that had the lion's heart. I had the luck to be called upon to give the roar!

MORALIST   It should not be supposed of all the millions who
marched to war in August, 1914, only a small proportion
went unwillingly away. The thrill of excitement ran through
the world, and the hearts of even the simplest masses
lifted to the trumpet-call. A prodigious event had happened. The monotony of toil and of the daily round was
suddenly broken. Everything was strange and new. War
aroused the primordial instincts of races born of strife. Adventure beckoned to her children. A larger, nobler life
seemed to be about to open upon the world. But it was,
in fact, only Death.

The only guide to a man is his conscience; the only
shield to his memory is the rectitude and sincerity of his
actions. It is very imprudent to walk through life without
this shield, because we are so often mocked by the failure
of our hopes and the upsetting of our calculations; but
with this shield, however the fates may play, we march
always in the ranks of honour.

IMPERIALIST   The year 1897, in the annals of the British people,
was marked by a declaration to the whole world of their
faith in the higher destinies of their race. If a strong man,
when the wine sparkles at the feast and the lights are
bright, boasts of his prowess, it is well he should have an
opportunity of showing in the cold and grey of the morning that he is no idle braggart. And unborn arbiters, with
a wider knowledge, and more developed brains, may trace
in recent events the influence of that mysterious Power
which, directing the progress of our species and regulating
the rise and fall of empires, has afforded that opportunity
to a people of whom at least it may be said that they have
added to the happiness, the learning and the liberties of
mankind.

We have passed an awful milestone in our history,
when the whole equilibrium of Europe has been deranged,
and the terrible words for the time being been pronounced
against the Western democracies: "Thou art weighed in

the balance and found wanting." And do not suppose that this is the end. This is only the beginning of the reckoning. This is only the first sip, the first foretaste of a bitter cup which will be proferred to us year by year unless, by a supreme recovery of moral health and martial vigour, we arise again and take our stand for freedom as in the olden time.

Let me, however, make this clear, in case there should be any mistake about it in any quarter. We mean to hold our own. I have not become the King's First Minister in order to preside over the liquidation of the British Empire. For that task, if ever it were prescribed, someone else would have to be found.

PRIME MINISTER

I would say to the House, as I said to those who have joined this government: "I have nothing to offer but blood, toil, tears and sweat."

We have before us an ordeal of the most grievous kind. We have before us many, many long months of struggle and suffering. You ask, what is our policy? I will say: it is to wage war, by sea, land and air, with all our might and with all the strength that God can give us: to wage war against a monstrous tyranny, never surpassed in the dark, lamentable catalogue of human crime. That is our policy. You ask, what is our aim? I can answer in one word: Victory—victory at all costs, victory in spite of all terror, victory, however long and hard the road may be; for without victory, there is no survival. Let that be realized; no survival for the British Empire; no survival for all that the British Empire has stood for, no survival for the urge and impulse of the ages, that mankind will move forward towards its goal. But I take up my task with buoyancy and hope. I feel sure that our cause will not be suffered to fail among men.

WAR LEADER   The Battle of France is over. I expect that the battle
of Britain is about to begin. Upon this battle depends the
survival of Christian civilization. Upon it depends our
own British life, and the long continuity of our institutions
and our Empire. The whole fury and might of the enemy
must very soon be turned on us. Hitler knows that he will
have to break us in this island or lose the war. If we can
stand up to him, all Europe may be free and the life of
the world may move forward into broad, sunlit uplands.
But if we fail, then the whole world including the United
States including all that we have known and cared for,
will sink into the abyss of a new Dark Age made more
sinister, and perhaps more protracted, by the lights of per-
verted science. Let us therefore brace ourselves to our duties, and so bear ourselves that, if the British Empire and
its Commonwealth last for a thousand years, men will
still say, "This was their finest hour."

The gratitude of every home in our island, in our
Empire, and indeed throughout the world, except in the
abodes of the guilty, goes out to the British airmen, who,
undaunted by odds, unwearied in their constant challenge
and mortal danger, are turning the tide of the world war
by their prowess and by their devotion. Never in the field
of human conflict was so much owed by so many to so
few.

We shall not flag or fail. We shall go on to the end,
we shall fight on the seas and oceans, we shall fight with
growing confidence and growing strength in the air, we
shall defend our island, whatever the cost may be, we
shall fight on the beaches, we shall fight on the landing
grounds, we shall fight in the fields and in the streets, we
shall fight in the hills; we shall never surrender.

We must never cease to proclaim in fearless tones the great principles of freedom and the rights of man which are the joint inheritance of the English-speaking world and which through Magna Carta, the Bill of Rights, the Habeas Corpus, trial by jury, and the English common law find their most famous expression in the American Declaration of Independence.

All this means that the people of any country have the right, and should have the power by constitutional action, by free unfettered elections, with secret ballot, to choose or change the character or form of government under which they dwell; that freedom of speech and thought should reign; that courts of justice, independent of the executive, unbiased by any party, should administer laws which have received the broad assent of large majorities or are consecrated by time and custom. Here are the title deeds of freedom which should lie in every cottage home.

WORLD
STATESMAN

Sir Winston Churchill died in 1965 at the age of ninety. A State funeral was held for him in St. Paul's Cathedral, London, and he was buried in the churchyard of Bladon Church, a small village just outside the Blenheim Palace Estate, the home of his ancestors.

INDEX

S